Anxiety Relief for Teen Girls

A Science-Backed Guide to Managing Social Stress, Panic, and Worry With CBT, Mindfulness, and Proven Strategies for Building Confidence and Inner Strength

Anya Dawson

Anya Dawson

Disclaimer Notice:

Please note the information contained within this document is for educational and entertainment purposes only. All effort has been executed to present accurate, up to date, reliable, complete information. No warranties of any kind are declared or implied. Readers acknowledge that the author is not engaged in the rendering of legal, financial, medical or professional advice. The content within this book has been derived from various sources. Please consult a licensed professional before attempting any techniques outlined in this book.

By reading this document, the reader agrees that under no circumstances is the author responsible for any losses, direct or indirect, that are incurred as a result of the use of the information contained within this document, including, but not limited to, errors, omissions, or inaccuracies.

Anya Dawson

Table of Contents

Anya Dawson

Introduction

I am thinking of you.

You are a brave girl, but sometimes, anxiety sneaks in and tries to convince you that you're not. It whispers doubts, makes your heart race, and fills your mind with endless "what-ifs." *What if I embarrass myself? What if they don't like me? What if I fail?* Anxiety loves to play these mind games, making you question yourself when, in reality, you are stronger than your anxiety.

Why Does Anxiety Affect Girls More?

If you feel like anxiety follows you around more than it does for the guys in your life—be it your father, brother, or friends—you're not imagining it. Research shows that teen girls are twice as likely to experience anxiety as boys (Chaplin et al., 2008). But why?

It's not because girls are weaker (let's shut that idea down right now). It's because of biology, society, and the pressure to be "perfect."

You, me, and all the girls around us tend to have a more active amygdala, the part of the brain that processes fear and emotions. That means your brain is *really good* at detecting threats—but sometimes, it reacts to everyday stress as if you're in real danger. On top of that, the world expects a lot from girls. You're told to be confident but not *too* confident. To be smart but not *too* outspoken. To be kind but not a pushover. It's exhausting.

Let's say you walk into school feeling okay, but then you hear your friends whispering. They glance in your direction, and suddenly, your brain starts spinning. *Are they talking about me? Did I do something wrong?* Your heart speeds up, your stomach tightens, and now you can't focus on anything else.

That's anxiety doing its thing—overanalyzing, jumping to conclusions, and making you doubt yourself. You don't have to live like this. Anxiety may be part of your story, but it doesn't get to be the author.

The Old Cherokee and His Granddaughter

Let me tell you a story.

A long time ago, an old Cherokee chief sat with his granddaughter and told her about the battle inside every person (Su'a, 2014):

"Inside each of us, there are two wolves," he said. "One is full of fear, anxiety, and self-doubt. It worries about everything and sees danger everywhere. The other wolf is strong, brave, and confident. It believes in itself, faces challenges head-on, and never lets fear hold it back. These two wolves are always fighting inside of you."

The granddaughter thought for a moment and asked, "Which wolf wins?"

The chief smiled. "The one you feed."

Right now, anxiety might feel like the loudest voice in your head, but it doesn't have to be the one you listen to. You get to decide which thoughts you feed. That's what this book is all about—learning how to stop feeding fear and start feeding confidence, courage, and strength.

How This Book Will Help You

There are a lot of books about anxiety, but this one is different. This book won't just tell you to "think positive" or "calm down" (because let's be real—when has that ever worked?). Instead, you'll get practical, science-backed strategies designed specifically for teen girls. These are techniques you can actually use when anxiety shows up.

You'll learn how to

- understand what's really happening in your brain when you feel anxious (hint: It's not your fault!).

- rewire anxious thoughts using cognitive behavioral therapy (CBT), the gold standard for anxiety treatment.

- use mindfulness in a way that actually helps (no sitting in silence for hours required!).

- handle panic attacks like a pro so they don't take over your life.

- set boundaries in friendships and relationships so you don't get stuck in anxiety-triggering situations.

This book is your toolkit—your guide to gaining confidence, managing stress, and finally feeling in control. Each chapter is packed with real-life strategies and step-by-step techniques to help you manage anxiety in different situations.

This Is Your Journey!

Anxiety might be part of your life, but guess what? It doesn't get to be in charge. It doesn't get to decide what you can or can't do. It doesn't get to hold you back from chasing your dreams, speaking your mind, or feeling truly confident in your own skin.

You are stronger. You are braver. You are more powerful than your worries want you to believe. And when you reach the final page, you'll possess this truth within you.

Anxiety doesn't get to write your story. You do.

So, take a deep breath, shake off the doubt, and let's get started.

Chapter 1: Anxiety 101—What's Happening in Your Brain?

Emma was only 13 when she first experienced anxiety, but at the time, she didn't understand what was happening to her. She would feel a sudden tightness in her chest, her hands would get clammy, and her thoughts would start racing uncontrollably. She assumed it was just stress or nerves, something everyone dealt with. But deep down, she knew something felt different.

When she was 15, she stumbled across an article about anxiety, and everything clicked. The feelings she had been experiencing for years had a name. The overwhelming worry, the restless nights, the moments where her heart pounded as if she were in danger—this was anxiety. It was both a relief and a shock. On one hand, she finally understood what was happening; on the other, she wondered why she hadn't known sooner.

This happens to so many people. When you don't know what you're experiencing, it's hard to find a way to manage it. You can't solve a problem you haven't defined. But once you name it, once you understand what anxiety is and why it happens, you can begin to take action. You can learn how to manage it, how to navigate through it, and how to make it less overwhelming.

In this chapter, let's break down exactly what's happening inside your mind when anxiety strikes. We'll take a look at the parts of your brain that are responsible for these feelings, why they react the way they do, and, most importantly, how understanding this process can help you manage it. Because the more you know about what's going on in your brain, the more power you have to handle it.

What Is Anxiety?

Anxiety is your body's natural response to stress, uncertainty, or fear. It is that nervous feeling you get before a big math test, when meeting new people, or while stepping into an unfamiliar situation.

What I want you to know here is that a little bit of anxiety is completely normal. In fact, small amounts of anxiety can even be helpful in keeping you alert, motivated, and ready to respond to important situations.

However, the problems start when anxiety becomes persistent and overwhelming, causing constant worry, fear, or physical symptoms like a racing heart, dizziness, shortness of breath, or trouble sleeping. Instead of helping you focus, it can make it harder to concentrate, enjoy things you usually love, or feel safe in situations that aren't actually dangerous.

When anxiety lingers for weeks or months, interferes with daily life, and leads to avoidance of everyday situations, it may be an *anxiety disorder*. Anxiety disorders can also bring intense physical symptoms like panic attacks, constant restlessness, and trouble sleeping, even when there's no immediate threat.

Did you know? Anxiety disorders are the most common mental health condition in the United States. Around 1 in 10 to 1 in 13 people experience anxiety, and about 8% of children and teens struggle with an anxiety disorder (Katzenstein, n.d.). You are not alone!

Looking Back in Time

I want you to take a trip down memory lane. Think back to when you were a little kid—what made you anxious? Maybe it was the dark, the monsters under your bed, or being away from your parents. Perhaps it was the first day of school, speaking in front of the class, or the fear of falling off your bike. Back then, your worries felt huge, but over time, you probably outgrew many of them.

Now that you're a teen, your triggers have changed. Instead of being afraid of what's hiding in the dark, you might worry about fitting in, doing well in school, or making big life decisions. Social situations, academic pressure, and the future can all feel overwhelming. The things that used to comfort you—like a nightlight or a hug from a parent—might not seem like enough anymore.

The good part is, just like you outgrew childhood fears, you can also learn to manage the anxieties you face now. Anxiety isn't just something that happens to you—it has a science behind it.

And to get started... drum roll, please! Let's get into the science of anxiety.

The Science of Anxiety

I know what you are thinking. *Another science lecture? No, thanks!* But trust me, this one's way more interesting because it's about you. And to make it fun, let's start with a scenario:

Imagine this: You're in the woods, enjoying the fresh air, maybe humming your favorite song, when suddenly—you freeze. A huge brown bear is standing right there in front of you. Its eyes lock onto yours. Your heart starts pounding like a drum solo, your palms get sweaty, and your legs feel like jelly. In that moment, your body is screaming "RUN!" or at least "DO SOMETHING!"

That intense reaction? That's anxiety in action—or, more specifically, your brain's **fight-or-flight** response kicking in.

Meet the Amygdala: Your Brain's Alarm System

The moment your eyes spot the bear, your amygdala (a tiny part of your brain responsible for detecting danger) goes into full panic mode (*The Biology of Anxiety*, n.d.). Think of it as the overprotective friend who freaks out at the slightest sign of trouble. The amygdala sends an urgent message to the rest of your brain, yelling, "ALERT! THREAT DETECTED!"

The Emergency Response Team: Hormones to the Rescue

Once your amygdala raises the alarm, your brain signals your body to release stress hormones like adrenaline and cortisol—kind of like pressing a big red emergency button. These chemicals flood your system, causing:

- **Racing heart:** Pumping more blood to your muscles so you can run faster (or fight, if necessary

- **Fast breathing:** Getting extra oxygen to power your escape

- **Sweaty palms:** Your body trying to cool down, just in case you need to sprint

- **Shaky legs:** Your muscles tensing, preparing to take action

All of this happens in seconds, before you've even had time to think about what to do. That's your fight-or-flight response—your body's way of keeping you alive in dangerous situations.

But What if There's No Bear?

Fight or flight, as the name suggests, is deciding whether to fight the threat or flee to safety (aka "Nope, I'm out!"). This response was super useful when humans had to escape wild animals in the past, but today, it can kick in during things like public speaking, exams, or awkward social situations—where running away isn't exactly an option.

Now, imagine you feel that same rush of anxiety... but instead of a bear, you're just sitting in class, staring at a test paper you completely forgot to study for. No actual life-or-death situation, but your brain doesn't know the difference.

The amygdala can't tell whether the "threat" is a wild animal or a math exam—it just reacts. So, even though there's no real danger, your body still releases stress hormones, making you feel shaky, sweaty, and on edge.

What Happens Next?

When your body goes into full-on fight-or-flight mode, you're ready to face danger head-on. But what happens after the initial surge of stress hormones? Once the danger (or imagined danger) has passed, your body needs to cool down and return to a relaxed state.

After the adrenaline rush, your parasympathetic nervous system—also known as the "rest-and-digest" system—takes over. Think of it as the off-switch for all the fight-or-flight chaos. Here's how it helps you calm down:

- **Heart rate slows:** Your heart no longer needs to pump at super speed. It gradually returns to its normal rhythm, which lowers your blood pressure and helps you feel calmer.

- **Breathing normalizes:** Those fast, shallow breaths slow down and become deeper, helping your body get rid of the extra adrenaline and bring things back to normal.

- **Muscles relax:** The tension in your muscles fades, and your body stops preparing for that big sprint. This makes you feel less shaky and more at ease.

- **Sweating stops:** Your body cools down, and the sweaty palms and clammy skin dry up as your temperature normalizes.

Breaking the Anxiety Habit

Your brain can also develop habits around anxiety. If you often feel anxious in certain situations (like giving a class presentation), your brain starts associating that situation with fear. Over time, even just thinking about doing it might trigger anxiety, even if there's no actual danger.

 This is where the prefrontal cortex (the logical, rational part of your brain) comes into play. It's the part of your brain that can help calm you down when anxiety kicks in (*The Biology of Anxiety*, n.d.). It gently suggests, "Hey, please take a deep breath. Think this through. You've been here before, and you survived." So, even though your amygdala (the alarm system) is going off, your prefrontal cortex is trying to calm it down.

I have good news: You can retrain your brain to break the anxiety cycle. By gradually exposing yourself to anxiety-inducing situations, you can teach your brain that there's no real threat. It's kind of like easing into cold water—you might feel overwhelmed at first, but over time, you'll realize it's not so bad. Do it more, and it gets easier. Your body and brain will learn that you don't need to panic, and those once-scary situations will start to feel more manageable.

In other words, while anxiety might try to hijack your brain, you've got the tools to retake control. With a little practice and patience, you can turn that fight-or-flight response into a calm and confident "I'm ready for this."

How Anxiety Manifests—Recognizing the Symptoms

Anxiety can show up in many different ways, and it's not always obvious. It's not just being a little nervous; it can create a whole spectrum of physical, emotional, and mental symptoms. But how do you know if what you're feeling is anxiety? Let's break down the signs so you can better understand when anxiety might be at play.

Physical Symptoms

Anxiety doesn't just mess with your mind; it affects your body, too. This happens because your body responds to anxiety with the same fight-or-flight mechanisms designed for real danger. Here are some of the most common physical symptoms:

- **Racing heart or palpitations:** You might feel like your heart is pounding, fluttering, or racing in your chest. This is your body preparing for action—either to fight or run away from the "danger" (real or perceived).

- **Shortness of breath:** It's common to feel like you can't get enough air, as if you're gasping for breath.

This happens because your body is trying to pump more oxygen to your muscles, preparing them for quick movement.

- **Sweating:** Anxiety often triggers sweating, particularly in your palms, forehead, or underarms. This is your body's way of cooling down in anticipation of running or fighting.

- **Muscle tension:** You may notice your muscles tightening up, especially in the neck, shoulders, or back. This tension can lead to aches and pains as your body prepares for physical action.

- **Dizziness or lightheadedness:** The rush of adrenaline can cause a feeling of dizziness or faintness. Your body diverts blood flow to your muscles, which can sometimes leave you feeling lightheaded or unsteady.

- **Shaking or trembling:** Your muscles may tremble or shake, particularly in your hands or legs. This is part of the body's fight-or-flight response as it readies itself for a physical reaction.

- **Dry mouth:** Anxiety can make your mouth feel dry, which happens when your body shuts down non-essential functions (like saliva production) to focus on survival.

- **Stomach upset:** While the "butterflies in your stomach" feeling is common, anxiety can also cause more severe digestive issues, such as nausea, diarrhea, or a feeling of tightness in the stomach. This happens because your digestive system slows down when you're anxious.

Emotional Symptoms

Beyond the physical effects, anxiety also has a big impact on your emotions. Here are some emotional symptoms you might experience:

- **Excessive worry:** One of the key signs of anxiety is constant, uncontrollable worry. You might find yourself thinking about worst-case scenarios or imagining problems that haven't even happened yet.

- **Restlessness:** Feeling on edge, fidgety, or like you just can't settle down is common with anxiety. It's as if your body is primed to react to a threat, but there's no actual threat in sight.

- **Irritability:** When anxiety takes over, it can make you feel easily irritated or frustrated, even by small things that wouldn't usually bother you. This is because anxiety takes up a lot of emotional energy, leaving you less patient and more sensitive.

- **Feelings of dread:** You might experience a constant sense of dread or fear that something bad is going to happen, even if you can't pinpoint why.

- **Fear of losing control:** It can make you feel powerless, overwhelmed, and even panicked as if you're no longer in charge of yourself or the situation.

Mental Symptoms

Your brain isn't immune to the effects of anxiety, either. Anxiety can cloud your thinking, making it hard to focus or process information clearly. Here are some mental symptoms that often accompany anxiety:

- **Difficulty concentrating:** Anxiety can make it hard to focus on tasks. Your mind might race through a million thoughts, all of them centered around worry or fear. Even the simplest tasks can start to feel daunting and unmanageable.

- **Racing thoughts:** Your mind may be flooded with a constant stream of thoughts, often about things that might go wrong or things you feel you have no control over. These racing thoughts can lead to mental exhaustion.

- **Constant fear of the future:** You may have an intense sense of fear about what might happen in the future. This can create a cycle of worrying about things that haven't happened yet, often without a real reason to be afraid.

- **Negative thinking patterns:** Anxiety can make you focus on worst-case scenarios, even when things are actually okay. You might catastrophize, imagining that things will go wrong in ways that are highly unlikely but still feel very real.

- **Difficulty sleeping:** Anxiety can interfere with sleep, either by making it hard to fall asleep or causing you to wake up in the middle of the night. Racing thoughts or physical symptoms, like a racing heart, can keep you up, making it harder to get the rest you need.

Behavioral Symptoms

When anxiety becomes persistent, it can affect the way you behave. Here's how it might influence your actions:

- **Avoidance:** You might start avoiding certain situations or places that make you anxious. This could be social events, public speaking, or anything that causes you stress. Over time, this avoidance can become more extreme, causing you to limit your life and opportunities.

- **Nervous habits:** Anxiety can lead to habits like biting your nails, tapping your foot, or pacing. These repetitive behaviors are ways your body tries to release the tension from anxiety.

- **Social withdrawal:** As anxiety can make social situations feel overwhelming, you might find yourself withdrawing from others. You may cancel plans or avoid being around people, further isolating yourself.

Are You Anxious?

It is time to take action! Let this simple body scan meditation activity be your guide in understanding your feelings of anxiousness. Next time, if anything triggers your anxiety, *name it to tame it.* Let's discuss some steps to find out what's making you anxious.

Set the Scene

- Find a comfortable, quiet space where you won't be disturbed for a few minutes.

- Sit or lie down in a relaxed position. You can choose a chair, a mat, or even your bed.

Close Your Eyes

- Close your eyes gently to minimize distractions, but if that feels uncomfortable, simply lower your gaze and soften your focus.

Start With Deep Breaths

- Take a deep breath in through your nose for a count of four. Hold for a second.

- Slowly breathe out through your mouth for a count of six.

- Repeat this breathing pattern two more times to help your body relax and focus on the present moment.

Focus on Your Feet

- Bring your attention to your feet. Are they tense? Do they feel cold, hot, or maybe even numb? Pay attention to what you feel. Notice if there's any discomfort, tension, or tightness in your feet.

- Gently move your toes, wiggle them a bit, and relax.

Move to Your Legs

- Now, focus on your legs. Are they relaxed or stiff? Do you feel any tension in your calves, thighs, or knees?

- Try to relax each leg, one at a time. Let go of any tightness or discomfort.

Check Your Stomach

- Move your attention up to your stomach. Are you feeling butterflies, tension, or even a tight knot in your belly?

- Breathe deeply into your belly, allowing it to expand with each inhale, and let it soften on each exhale.

Scan Your Chest and Heart

- Bring your focus to your chest. Does your heart feel like it's pounding, or is your breathing shallow? Notice if you're holding your breath or if your chest feels tight.

- Take slow, deep breaths into your chest, letting the breath expand fully before exhaling.

Relax Your Shoulders and Neck

- Now, focus on your shoulders. Are they raised up toward your ears, or do they feel heavy? Move your attention to your neck. Are you feeling any tension or stiffness here?

- Gently roll your shoulders backward and forward a few times to release any tightness.

Notice Your Hands and Arms

- Check in with your hands and arms. Are your hands clenched into fists, or do your palms feel sweaty? Are your arms relaxed or tense?

- Relax your hands, stretch your fingers out, and notice how your arms feel.

Scan Your Face

- Now, focus on your face. Are your jaw or lips clenched? Are your eyes squinting or wide open? Is your forehead furrowed with tension?

- Unclench your jaw, let your tongue rest lightly in your mouth, and soften your facial muscles. Try to release any tension here.

Take One Final Deep Breath

- Now, take a final slow, deep breath in, and exhale gently. Let your body relax fully as you notice how you feel overall.

How Do You Feel?

After finishing the scan, take a moment to check in with yourself. How did you feel during the scan? Did you notice areas of your body that felt tense or tight? Were there signs of anxiety, such as a racing heart, shallow breathing, or muscle tension?

Pro tip: If possible, grab a journal or notebook and write down what you felt in your body during the meditation. Where did you notice tension? When do you usually feel these sensations in daily life?

Time to Check Yourself!

You've made it through this chapter—well done! Now, before we jump into the next one, let's take a moment to check in with what you've learned. Here's a little self-check to see how well you're tuned in to your own anxiety:

- When you feel nervous, do you notice physical signs like a racing heart, sweaty palms, or shallow breathing?

- Have you ever felt like your thoughts are spinning out of control, making it hard to focus on anything else?

- Can you recall a time when you felt anxious but weren't sure why?

If you said yes to any of these, don't worry—that's your brain doing its thing! Anxiety is a natural response, and now that you know how to recognize it, you're one step closer to understanding how to handle it.

In the next chapter, we're going to get into the different types of anxiety and figure out which one feels the most like you. Ready to find out more about what's going on inside your brain? Let's go!

Chapter 2: Different Types of Anxiety—Which One Feels Like You?

Inside Out has always been one of my favorite movies because of how brilliantly it captures the way emotions work in our minds. But when *Inside Out 2* introduced anxiety as one of Riley's new emotions, it felt even more real.

As Riley enters her teenage years, she faces new pressures—making the hockey team, impressing her new friends, and figuring out who she wants to be. Anxiety, the newest addition to her mind's control center, tries to keep her prepared for every possible failure. At first, it seems helpful—reminding her to work harder, practice more, and avoid mistakes. But soon, anxiety takes over completely. Instead of helping Riley, it overwhelms her with worries about what might go wrong until she spirals into her first panic attack.

That moment is powerful because it captures exactly how anxiety can feel—like a runaway train of thoughts you can't stop. As Jenny, one of the film's creators, put it, "As Riley and Anxiety launched into this spiral in tandem, I knew on such a deeply personal level what that was like" (Comiter, 2024).

But Riley's journey also shows something important: Anxiety isn't the enemy. It's there to protect her, to prepare her for challenges. The problem comes when it drowns out everything else and makes her feel like she's constantly on edge. And that's the tricky part—sometimes, anxiety feels like it's helping when really, it's keeping you stuck in a cycle of fear.

In this chapter, we're going to break down different types of anxiety, starting with the one Riley experiences: Generalized anxiety—when your brain is always in "what if" mode, even when there's no real danger. If you've ever found yourself overthinking the worst possible outcome in everyday situations, this might sound familiar. Let's dive in and see which version of anxiety feels like you.

Different Types of Anxiety

Anxiety shows up in different ways for different people— some feel constant worry, others as a sudden wave of panic, and some as a fear that holds them back from everyday activities.

We will be taking a closer look at different types, but with a twist. To make things relatable, we'll discuss a classroom where different students experience anxiety in their own unique ways. Through their stories, you'll see how anxiety can affect people differently—and maybe even recognize parts of your own experience along the way.

Generalized Anxiety Disorder

Have you ever felt worried for no obvious reason? Like your brain is playing a never-ending list of things that could go wrong, even when everything seems fine? That's what life can feel like for someone with generalized anxiety disorder (GAD). It's not just feeling anxious once in a while—it's a persistent feeling of worry or dread that sticks around, even when there's no clear reason for it.

What Is GAD?

GAD is a type of anxiety that causes excessive, uncontrollable worry about everyday things. It feels like your brain is constantly stuck in a loop of imagining worst-case scenarios and stressing over things that might not even happen. This worry can show up at any time, not just during stressful situations, and it can make even normal daily activities feel exhausting.

Symptoms of GAD

People with GAD might experience:

- **Excessive worry:** Constantly thinking about things that might go wrong, even small things

- **Restlessness:** A constant sense of unease or difficulty relaxing

- **Difficulty concentrating:** Trouble focusing because your mind is racing with worries

- **Sleep problems:** Lying awake at night, overthinking every little detail of the day

- **Physical symptoms:** Headaches, stomach aches, or muscle tension for no clear reason

Common Triggers for GAD

Anxiety can latch onto almost anything, but some common triggers for teen girls include:

- **School and grades:** Worrying about tests, assignments, or not being "good enough"

- **Friendships and social pressure:** Overanalyzing conversations or fearing rejection

- **The future:** Constantly stressing about life after school, career choices, or failure

- **Everyday situations:** Feeling anxious about being late, forgetting homework, or saying the wrong thing

Brian's Story: The Straight-A Student Who Couldn't Turn Off His Worry

Brian is one of the top students in his class. He gets straight A's, always turns in his homework on time, and is the person everyone assumes has it all figured out. But what his classmates don't see is what happens when he goes home.

After school, Brian sits in his room, staring at his test paper—he got a 95%. But instead of feeling proud, his stomach sinks. *Why didn't I get 100?* He starts obsessing over the one question he missed, wondering if it means he's slipping.

That night, he lies awake in bed, staring at the ceiling. His mind spins through everything that could go wrong:

- *What if I fail the next test?*

- *What if I don't get accepted into a great college?*

- *What if my friends think I'm annoying and just pretend to like me?*

Even when Brian has nothing to worry about, his brain creates worries. It's like his mind is constantly trying to solve problems that don't exist, which leaves him drained and exhausted.

Eventually, Brian confides in his school counselor, who helps him understand that his anxiety is playing tricks on him. She teaches him grounding techniques, like deep breathing and writing down his worries to fact-check them later. Over time, Brian learns that his thoughts aren't always reality—and that he deserves rest, even if he isn't perfect.

What Brian's Story Teaches Us

GAD makes your mind work overtime, stressing over things that might not even happen. But just like Brian, recognizing the signs of anxiety and reaching out for help can make a huge difference. Anxiety might be loud, but it doesn't have to control you.

Social Anxiety

Ever felt like all eyes were on you, just waiting for you to mess up? Maybe your heart started pounding before speaking in class, or you overanalyzed something you said to a friend, convinced they secretly thought it was weird. If that sounds familiar, you're not alone. Social anxiety disorder (SAD) is one of the most common types of anxiety, and it makes social situations feel overwhelming—even ones that seem totally normal to other people.

What Is Social Anxiety?

Social anxiety disorder is more than just feeling shy. It's an intense fear of being judged, embarrassed, or humiliated in front of others. People with social anxiety often avoid situations where they have to interact with others, especially when they might be the center of attention. It can make even simple things—like answering a question in class, ordering food at a restaurant, or joining a group conversation—feel terrifying.

Symptoms of Social Anxiety

If you have social anxiety, you might experience:

- **Extreme self-consciousness:** Feeling like everyone is watching and judging you

- **Fear of embarrassment:** Worrying that you'll say or do something awkward

- **Avoidance of social situations:** Skipping events, conversations, or even school to avoid feeling anxious

- **Physical symptoms:** Racing heart, sweating, shaking, blushing, nausea, or feeling dizzy when in social settings

- **Overanalyzing interactions:** Replaying conversations and assuming you said something wrong

Common Triggers for Social Anxiety

Some common triggers of social anxiety are:

- **Speaking in class:** Answering a question or giving a presentation

- **Meeting new people:** Struggling to start or maintain conversations

- **Group settings:** Worrying about how others perceive you in social situations

- **Being the center of attention:** Feeling panicked when others look at you

- **Social media pressure:** Overthinking how you come across online or stressing over likes and comments

Scarlet's Story: The Girl Who Wanted to Disappear

Scarlet has always been quiet, but lately, it feels like her shyness has turned into something bigger. Every morning, she dreads school—not because of the classes, but because of the social interactions.

During English class, her teacher calls on her to read a passage aloud. Her hands start to sweat, her heart races, and she suddenly feels like she might forget how to read altogether. *What if my voice shakes? What if I mess up?* she thinks. When she finally speaks, she rushes through the passage, barely breathing. Even though she gets through it, her mind replays every tiny mistake for the rest of the day.

At lunch, Scarlet sits with her friends but barely speaks. She wants to join the conversation, but the words get stuck in her throat. *What if I say something dumb? What if no one cares what I have to say?* Instead, she just nods along, pretending she's fine.

One day, Scarlet's best friend notices how quiet she's been and asks if she's okay. After some hesitation, Scarlet admits how anxious she feels in social situations. Her friend reassures her that she's not alone and encourages her to talk to the school counselor. Over time, Scarlet starts using small strategies—like deep breathing before speaking and reminding herself that people aren't judging her as harshly as she thinks. It's still a challenge, but she's learning that she doesn't have to be perfect to be part of the conversation.

What Scarlet's Story Teaches Us

Social anxiety makes everyday interactions feel like a performance with the whole world watching. But the truth is, most people are focused on themselves—not analyzing your every move. If social anxiety holds you back, small steps—like practicing conversations, challenging negative thoughts, or talking to someone you trust—can make a huge difference.

Panic Disorder

Suppose you're sitting in class, feeling totally fine one moment, and then suddenly, out of nowhere, your heart starts racing, your chest feels tight, and you can't catch your breath. Your hands shake, your stomach turns, and for a terrifying few minutes, you feel like something really bad is happening—like you might pass out, lose control, or even die. Then, just as quickly as it came, the feeling starts to fade, leaving you exhausted and confused.

This is the sensation of a panic attack. For those with panic disorder, these attacks can occur unexpectedly, which makes them anxious about when the next one might happen.

What Is Panic Disorder?

Panic disorder is a form of anxiety in which a person experiences frequent and unpredictable panic attacks. These episodes can feel overwhelming and intense, often making people worry that something is physically wrong with them. Because panic attacks feel so scary, people with Panic Disorder may start avoiding situations where they fear another attack might happen.

Symptoms of Panic Attacks

When a panic attack hits, it can feel overwhelming. Your body may respond with physical symptoms like a rapid heartbeat or pounding chest, making it seem like your heart is racing or skipping beats. You might feel short of breath, like you can't get enough air, or experience dizziness and lightheadedness. Sweating, trembling, or shaking are also common, along with nausea or stomach discomfort. Some people describe a sense of doom, as if something terrible is about to happen, while others may feel detached from reality—like they're watching themselves from the outside. The fear of losing control or even dying can make it even scarier, even though you're actually safe.

Common Triggers for Panic Attacks

Panic attacks can be triggered by stress or situations that feel overwhelming. Crowded places or tight spaces might make them worse, and sometimes, too much caffeine or sugar can set them off. The fear of having another panic attack, known as "fear of the fear," can also be a trigger. Big life changes, like moving to a new school or preparing for an important test, can heighten anxiety. And sometimes, panic attacks seem to come out of nowhere, with no clear reason at all.

Dylan's Story: The Boy Who Feared His Own Body

Dylan is a brilliant student. He always performs well in school and seems to have everything under control—until one day, in the middle of a math test, something terrifying happens.

Out of nowhere, his chest tightens, and his heart starts racing like he just ran a mile. His hands shake, and his breath comes in short gasps. He feels dizzy, like he might pass out. His mind starts spiraling: *What's happening? Am I having a heart attack? Am I dying?*

He bolts out of the classroom and rushes to the nurse's office. The nurse checks his vitals and reassures him that physically, he's fine. But Dylan isn't convinced—how could something that felt that real not be dangerous?

After that day, Dylan starts fearing another attack. He avoids taking tests and sitting in crowded rooms. He stops drinking coffee, thinking that might have caused it. But the more he tries to avoid it, the more anxious he feels.

Eventually, Dylan talks to his sister, who explains that what he experienced was a panic attack—a false alarm sent by his brain's fight-or-flight system. Over time, Dylan learns that panic attacks, while scary, aren't dangerous. By facing his fear instead of avoiding it, he starts to take back control of his life.

What Dylan's Story Teaches Us

Panic attacks can feel overwhelming, but they are not dangerous. They are temporary waves of intense anxiety that always pass—even if they don't feel like they will in the moment. Understanding this and learning how to calm your body can help you manage Panic Disorder if it's something you experience.

Specific Phobias

We all have things we're afraid of. Maybe it's a creepy spider in the corner of the room or the thought of speaking in front of a class. But for some people, these fears are much more intense and can interfere with everyday life. This is called specific phobia, where someone experiences a strong, irrational fear of a specific situation, object, or animal.

What Are Specific Phobias?

Specific phobias are extreme, uncontrollable fears of certain objects, situations, or activities. The fear is much stronger than the actual danger involved. Even if someone knows their fear doesn't make sense, they still struggle to control it.

People with specific phobias often know that their fear is out of proportion to the actual danger, but that doesn't make it any less real. These fears can lead to avoiding certain situations or places altogether, which can affect school, friendships, and even future opportunities.

Common Types of Specific Phobias

There are various types of specific phobias, each with its own set of triggers and manifestations:

Animal phobias, for example, involve intense fears of certain animals, often rooted in past traumatic experiences or cultural influences. For instance, cynophobia is the fear of dogs, usually stemming from a negative encounter, while arachnophobia—the fear of spiders—can be tied to evolutionary instincts that associate spiders with danger.

Another common animal-related phobia is ophidiophobia, or the fear of snakes, which may be linked to the danger portrayed in popular culture.

Natural environment phobias, like acrophobia (fear of heights), are triggered by the body's instinctual response to potential threats from high places, which can cause dizziness or panic. Thalassophobia, the fear of deep water, taps into the fear of the unknown lurking beneath the surface. Similarly, astraphobia, or the fear of thunderstorms, often leads to extreme anxiety during storms and avoidance behaviors.

Situational phobias can also significantly disrupt daily life. Aviophobia, or fear of flying, prevents some individuals from traveling by air, while claustrophobia—fear of enclosed spaces—can make elevators or tunnels feel unbearable. Vehophobia, or fear of driving, is often rooted in past accidents or anxiety over losing control on the road.

Blood-injection-injury phobias are centered around medical procedures and can include trypanophobia, the fear of needles, and hemophobia, the fear of blood. People with these phobias may experience severe anxiety or even faint at the sight of blood or a needle.

Nosocomephobia, the fear of hospitals, is often linked to past trauma or a fear of illness.

There are also more unusual phobias, like **coulrophobia**, the fear of clowns, which may be triggered by their exaggerated facial expressions or unpredictable nature. **Mysophobia**, or fear of germs, can lead to obsessive cleaning or avoidance of public places, while **phonophobia**, the fear of loud noises, can make sounds like alarms or fireworks deeply distressing.

Phobias can range from mild discomfort to severe panic attacks, and they often develop due to personal experiences, cultural influences, or even genetics. The good news? With time, exposure therapy, and support, many people learn to manage or even overcome their fears!

Jessica's Story: The Girl Who Avoided Class Presentations

Jessica is an outgoing student—she loves hanging out with friends and can talk for hours about her favorite TV shows. But the moment a teacher says the words "class presentation," her stomach drops.

Jessica has glossophobia, a fear of public speaking. Just the thought of standing in front of the class makes her heart pound and her hands shake. The last time she had to present, her voice cracked, and she felt like she couldn't breathe. She was convinced everyone was judging her.

To avoid going through that again, Jessica starts skipping class whenever presentations are due. She makes up excuses, asks her teacher if she can submit a written report instead, and even pretends to be sick. But the more she avoids speaking in front of others, the worse her fear gets.

Finally, her English teacher pulls her aside and suggests practicing in small steps—first speaking in front of a mirror, then reading out loud to a friend, and eventually trying to present in class for just a few seconds at a time. Slowly,

Jessica realizes that while she still feels nervous, she can handle it.

What Jessica's Story Teaches Us

Phobias can feel paralyzing, but avoiding them only makes them stronger. The best way to overcome a specific phobia is to face it in small steps, just like Jessica did.

Health Anxiety

Health anxiety, also known as illness anxiety disorder (previously called hypochondria), is the excessive worry about having a serious medical condition, even when there's no real reason to be concerned. People with health anxiety often misinterpret normal body sensations—like a headache, a racing heart, or a slight cough—as signs of a severe illness.

Symptoms of Health Anxiety

Some common symptoms that can represent health anxiety include:

- constantly checking your body for unusual symptoms

- googling minor symptoms and convincing yourself it's something serious

- feeling anxious after hearing about diseases or medical conditions

- seeking reassurance from doctors, family, or friends but still worrying afterward

- avoiding hospitals, medical TV shows, or anything related to illness

Common Triggers

So, what triggers health anxiety? It can include:

- reading or hearing about diseases in the news or online

- experiencing a mild symptom (like a headache) and fearing it's something life-threatening

- having a family member who has been seriously ill

- a past experience with a health scare, even if it turned out to be nothing

Maya and the Google Spiral

Maya was a healthy 16-year-old, but anytime she felt even the slightest headache or stomach pain, her mind went into overdrive. One night, after feeling a tightness in her chest, she searched online and found articles about heart conditions. Even though she was young and had no risk factors, she convinced herself something was seriously wrong. She kept checking her pulse, asked her mom repeatedly if she should go to the ER, and couldn't sleep from the worry.

Her parents took her to the doctor, who reassured her that she was perfectly healthy. But even after that, the cycle continued—every new symptom led to another Google search, more anxiety, and more doctor visits. It wasn't until she learned about health anxiety and how it works that she started to recognize the pattern. By focusing on facts, limiting internet searches, and practicing grounding techniques, Maya slowly learned to manage her worries instead of letting them control her.

Health anxiety can feel overwhelming, but with the right tools and support, it can get better.

Which One Feels Like You?

To help identify which type of anxiety you might be going through, let's do an activity.

Step 1: Pay Attention to Your Anxiety

The next time you feel anxious, pause and observe what's happening. Take a moment to write down your symptoms in your journal or use the notes app on your phone. Ask yourself:

- *What physical sensations am I feeling?* These could include heart racing, sweating, stomachache, or dizziness.

- *What thoughts are going through my mind?* Ask yourself: *Am I overthinking, worrying about the worst-case scenario, or feeling out of control?*

- *What triggered this feeling?* It might be a test, social situation, certain object, or something else.

Step 2: Match Your Symptoms to an Anxiety Type

Now, go back to the different types of anxiety listed earlier. Which one sounds the most like what you experienced?

- Is your worry constant and about everything? This could be a sign of generalized anxiety disorder.

- Do social situations make you feel panicked or self-conscious? That might be social anxiety.

- Did your anxiety come out of nowhere with strong physical symptoms? This could be panic disorder.

- Was it triggered by a specific fear, like heights or needles? That sounds like a specific phobia.

- Were you convinced you were seriously ill even when nothing was wrong? This could be health anxiety.

It's possible to relate to more than one type—anxiety isn't always just one thing! The more you understand your own patterns, the easier it becomes to manage them.

Step 3: Reflect and Take Action

Now that you've identified your anxiety type (or types), think about these questions:

- What patterns do you notice?

- Are certain triggers making your anxiety worse?

- What small steps could help you manage these feelings better? Is it a breathing exercise, talking to someone, or challenging anxious thoughts?

Understanding your anxiety is the first step toward taking control of it. The more aware you are, the better you can handle it.

Once you know the type of anxiety you are going through, we will go through ways to challenge and change anxious thinking in the next chapter!

Chapter 3: Rewriting Your Anxiety Script (CBT Strategies)

For a moment, I want you to imagine you are directing a movie. You control the script, the scenes, and the way every moment unfolds. But what if your script is full of worst-case scenarios, fear, and self-doubt? If that is the story playing in your mind, it's easy to believe it's real—even when it's not.

Now, picture yourself sitting in the director's chair, watching two different versions of the same scene play out on the big screen.

Version one is the anxious script where the main character, which is you, sends a text to a friend. Minutes pass. No reply. The camera zooms in on your face, eyes darting, fingers tapping anxiously. The background music shifts—tense, uncertain. Your mind starts scripting a dramatic narrative: *She's avoiding me. She must be so mad at me. I must have messed up somehow.* Flashbacks of past conversations play as evidence, and before you know it, the scene spirals into rejection and loneliness.

Version two is a balanced script with the same scene. It's the same text, but this time, the background music is calm. You watch your phone, then shrug and move on with your day. Your mind offers a different narrative: *She's probably busy. She'll text back later.* Instead of fixating on the unknown, this version of the script gives room for possibilities—ones that don't lead to unnecessary stress.

Both versions start with the same moment. The only difference is the way the story is told.

But since you are the director here, you don't have to stick to the anxious script. YOU have the power to rewrite it! When the movie is in full action—when your mind is racing, and the script is filled with worst-case scenarios—this is where cognitive behavioral therapy (CBT) steps in. It helps you pause, review the storyline, and decide if it actually makes sense. CBT teaches you how to catch those anxious thoughts before they spiral, question whether they're really true, and replace them with a more balanced, realistic perspective.

You wouldn't let a bad first draft become the final cut, right? In this chapter, you'll learn how to recognize the unhelpful stories your mind tells you and rewrite them into something that serves you instead of stresses you. Let's get started.

What Is Cognitive Behavioral Therapy?

CBT is a type of therapy that helps people manage anxiety, stress, and other emotional challenges by breaking down overwhelming problems into smaller, more manageable parts. It's based on the idea that our thoughts, feelings, and behaviors are all connected—meaning if we change one, we can influence the others.

The Five Main Areas of CBT

CBT breaks down problems into five main areas that are interconnected. Understanding each area helps you better manage your thoughts, feelings, and actions, leading to healthier emotional responses and more productive behaviors.

1. Situations: What's Happening Around You?

The first area is the situation itself. In CBT, the situation refers to the event or circumstance happening around you in the present moment. These situations can be external (things happening in your environment) or internal (your own thoughts or physical sensations). They are often the initial trigger for a cycle of thoughts, emotions, physical reactions, and behaviors. However, what's critical to understand is that it's not the situation itself that causes your emotional response but how you interpret or perceive it.

External Situations

External situations are real-world events or circumstances that are happening around you. It could be anything from social situations, work-related stress and interactions with others to environmental factors. The key is that the external situation activates certain thoughts and feelings.

Some examples of external situations include:

- entering a room full of strangers at a party or event

- being stuck in a traffic jam and running late for an important appointment

- a friend canceling plans you were excited about

- receiving a text message or phone call from a loved one asking to talk

Internal Situations

Internal situations can be just as triggering as external ones. These might involve thoughts, physical sensations, or memories that arise within your mind and body. Internal situations often stem from self-reflection or personal anxieties and can be a trigger for emotional and behavioral responses.

Internal situations can include:

- a racing heart that arises when you're thinking about something stressful

- a critical thought about your appearance or abilities when you see yourself in the mirror

- negative self-talk that starts in your mind when you're about to take on a new challenge

The Role of Perception

How you perceive the situation is essential in CBT. Two people can experience the same situation but react to it differently because they interpret it in different ways. One person might feel excited and optimistic about a new work opportunity, while another might feel nervous and inadequate due to past failures or self-doubt. The difference lies in the cognitive filter through which each person views the world.

So, understanding that situations are the initial triggers is essential because it allows you to pinpoint where and how to intervene in the thought-feeling-behavior Cycle. Often, individuals become focused on trying to control their emotions or behaviors in a given situation, but the real change begins by examining the situation itself—specifically, how we perceive and interpret it.

2. Thoughts: What Are You Telling Yourself?

The second key area in CBT is thoughts—the internal dialogue or commentary we have in response to a situation. These are the mental statements or beliefs we automatically generate about what's happening around us, and they often shape how we feel and behave.

Understanding Thoughts

Thoughts can be helpful, neutral, or unhelpful, and in CBT, we focus on identifying those that are irrational, distorted, or unhelpful. These negative or distorted thoughts tend to exaggerate situations, leading to heightened anxiety, fear, and avoidance. Unhelpful thoughts often feed into emotional distress, like anxiety or depression, and can trigger problematic behaviors like avoidance or overreaction.

You can either have **automatic thoughts**, which are quick, knee-jerk reactions to situations. They happen so quickly that we often don't realize we're thinking them, yet they influence how we feel and act. Or you can fall for **cognitive**

distortions, which are patterns of thought that consistently lead to negative thinking. Cognitive distortions are common and are often biased or unrealistic, contributing to unnecessary stress or anxiety.

Common Cognitive Distortions

Let's explore some common cognitive distortions that can negatively affect our thinking:

Catastrophizing occurs when your mind automatically assumes the worst possible outcome, even if it's highly unlikely. This thinking pattern magnifies problems and makes them feel overwhelming and impossible to handle. For example, if you're about to give a presentation at school, you might think, *If I mess up, my classmates will laugh at me, and I will never be able to face them again.* In reality, making a mistake is unlikely to have such extreme consequences, but catastrophizing makes it feel inevitable. This type of thinking fuels anxiety and can make it difficult to take risks or try new things.

All-or-nothing thinking, also called black-and-white thinking, is when you view situations in extremes—either something is a total success or an absolute failure, with no gray area. If things don't go perfectly, they're perceived as a disaster. A student who gets a few answers wrong on a test might think, *If I don't get every question right, I'm not smart enough.* This kind of rigid thinking makes it easy to feel discouraged and overlook progress, even when you've done well overall.

Overgeneralization happens when you take one bad experience and assume it will always be that way. If you fail a math test, you might think, *I'll never be good at math*. One mistake suddenly feels like proof that you'll always struggle. This kind of thinking makes it hard to stay motivated because it convinces you that past failures will keep happening, even when that's not true.

Mind reading is when you assume you know what others are thinking—usually in a negative way—without any actual proof. This can make social situations stressful. If you send a text to a friend and they don't reply right away, you might think, *They must be mad at me* or *They don't really like me*. In reality, they could just be busy, but mind reading leads to self-doubt and unnecessary worry, making friendships and social interactions more difficult.

Filtering is when you focus only on the negative parts of a situation while ignoring anything positive. It's like having a mental filter that blocks out anything good. If you work hard on a school project and get a lot of praise, but one classmate makes a small critique, you might think, *Everyone must have hated it*. This kind of thinking makes it hard to feel good about your accomplishments and can lower your confidence over time.

Personalization is when you blame yourself for things that aren't actually your fault. If your group loses a soccer game, you might think, *It's all my fault because I missed that goal*. Even though it was a team effort, personalization makes you feel responsible for things beyond your control. This can lead to guilt and make you feel like you're always falling short, even when you're not.

Recognizing these thinking traps is the first step in challenging them. Once you catch yourself falling into these patterns, you can start replacing them with more balanced and realistic thoughts.

3. Emotions: How Do You Feel?

Your emotions are the next big piece of the puzzle. Emotions are how you feel in response to your thoughts, and they can be *really* powerful. Sometimes, it feels like emotions just take over out of nowhere, but in reality, they're often triggered by what you're thinking in that moment.

Here's where CBT comes in: The first step to changing how you feel is recognizing that your emotions follow your thoughts. If your thoughts are making you feel awful, the good news is that you *can* change them! Instead of thinking *Everyone is going to think I'm weird*, during a speech, you could reframe it as:

- *Most people are focused on their own stuff, not analyzing my every move.*

- *Even if I mess up, I'll survive. People forget small mistakes fast.*

- *I've prepared for this. I might even do great!*

Shifting your thoughts like this can take the edge off your emotions, helping you feel calmer and more in control. The more you practice, the easier it gets! Instead of letting your emotions run the show, you'll learn how to manage them in a way that makes life *so much* less stressful.

4. Physical Feelings: What Does Your Body Do?

Your body reacts to emotions in all sorts of ways—even when you don't realize it. These physical feelings, or physiological responses, happen automatically when you experience certain emotions. Think of it as your body's way of trying to protect you, even if the "danger" isn't real.

For example, if you're feeling nervous before a party, your body might react with sweaty palms, a racing heart, or even an upset stomach. If you've ever felt butterflies in your stomach before speaking in class or shaky hands before sending a risky text, that's your body responding to stress. Sometimes, these reactions can be overwhelming—like when your heart pounds so hard it feels like everyone in the room can hear it.

How CBT Can Help

These physical reactions often reinforce your emotional state. If your heart is racing and your hands are shaking, your brain might think, *See? I knew this situation was scary!*—which makes you feel even *more* anxious. But here's the thing: Just like thoughts influence emotions, you can also work backward by calming your body first.

5. Actions: How Do You React?

Your actions are the final piece of the puzzle—how you behave in response to your thoughts, emotions, and physical feelings. The way you react can either reinforce the cycle of negative thoughts and feelings or help you break free from them.

Let's say you're feeling anxious about a party. Your thoughts are telling you, *I'll embarrass myself* or *No one will want to talk to me.* Your body is responding with a tight chest and a nervous stomach. So, what do you do? Maybe you decide to cancel at the last minute and stay home. This is called avoidance behavior, and while it might feel like relief in the moment, it actually makes anxiety worse in the long run.

Why? Every time you avoid something that makes you anxious, your brain learns: *Yep, that was definitely dangerous.* Next time, the fear will feel even bigger, making it even harder to face.

How CBT Can Help

Instead of letting avoidance take over, CBT teaches you to gradually face your fears. This is called graded exposure, and it helps you build confidence step by step.

For example, if going to a big party feels too overwhelming, you could

- start with a small hangout with one or two friends.

- challenge negative thoughts. For example, think: *Maybe I won't embarrass myself. Maybe people will be nice.*

- go to the party but set a small goal, like staying for 30 minutes or talking to one new person.

By taking small steps instead of avoiding situations, you'll train your brain to see that the things you fear aren't actually as scary as they seem. Over time, this helps you feel braver and more in control, so fear doesn't get to make your decisions for you!

How Thoughts Shape Feelings and Actions

Anxiety often feels overwhelming, but at its core, it follows a predictable pattern:

- A **thought** triggers a **feeling**, which leads to an **action**.

This process is known as the thought-feeling-behavior cycle, and it plays a powerful role in shaping our experiences. How we interpret a situation shapes our feelings, which then impact our responses. By changing the way we think, we can alter how we feel and behave.

Understanding this cycle is key to breaking free from unhelpful thought patterns and reducing anxiety. Let's explore how this works in real life:

When Anxious Thoughts Take Over

Suppose you just got a text from a friend inviting you to a party this weekend. You should feel excited, but instead, your stomach tightens. Social situations make you nervous, and before you even have time to think, your brain jumps into panic mode.

You get an anxious **thought**: *Everyone at the party will think I'm weird.*

Now, how do you **feel**? Nervous? Embarrassed? Maybe sick to your stomach? Your heart starts pounding, and just thinking about walking into that party makes your skin crawl. So, you do what feels safest: You avoid it.

As a **behavior** response, you stare at the message for a while, then type: "Sorry, I have a lot of homework. Maybe next time!"

The moment you hit send, you feel relief. Phew. Crisis averted. No awkward small talk. No embarrassing moments.

But later that night, you scroll through your feed and see pictures from the party. Your friends are laughing, having fun. And suddenly, that relief turns into something else: regret.

You wonder, *What if I had gone? Would it have been that bad? Am I missing out?* But it's too late. Anxiety convinced you to sit this one out, and now, it feels like everyone is getting closer while you're stuck on the sidelines.

And here's the tricky part: Next time you get invited somewhere, the same anxious thought pops up, only stronger. *Remember last time? You avoided it, and nothing bad happened. Just do that again!*

And so, the cycle continues. Avoidance feels like protection, but really, it's just fear keeping you stuck.

But what if you could break that cycle? What if you could rewrite that thought and create a different outcome?

Let's try it:

1. Replace your old thought with a new thought: *I might feel awkward at first, but most people are too busy worrying about themselves to judge me.*

2. Replace your old feeling with a new feeling: Still a little nervous—of course! That's normal. But now, there's also a tiny spark of confidence.

3. Replace your old behavior with new behavior: Instead of making an excuse, type: "That sounds fun! What time are you going?"

The day of the party, you still feel butterflies in your stomach. But you remind yourself: *I don't have to be perfect. I just have to show up.* At first, yeah, it's a little awkward. But then there is a slow shift. You find a friend, start talking, laugh at a joke. Someone compliments your outfit. The music is good. And guess what? You're actually... having fun. Later that night, when you check your phone, there's no regret. Instead, you think, I'm really glad I went.

And the next time you get invited somewhere? Saying yes feels just a little bit easier.

This is how we break the cycle—not by forcing ourselves to be fearless but by giving ourselves the chance to see that maybe, just maybe, our anxious thoughts aren't always right.

Why This Matters

Your thoughts shape your reality. If you constantly tell yourself negative stories, you'll experience the world through that lens—full of fear, doubt, and worst-case scenarios. But if you learn to challenge and change your thoughts, you can rewrite your internal narrative into one that builds confidence and resilience.

Not every thought that comes to mind needs to be taken as truth. You are the director of your own mental script, so why not make it one that supports you instead of holding you back?

CBT Techniques to Calm Your Mind and Body

When stress, anxiety, or overwhelming emotions take over, it can feel like you've lost control. Your heart races, your thoughts spiral, and your body tenses up. But here's the truth: You have more control than you think.

Cognitive behavioral therapy teaches powerful techniques to help you calm both your mind and body. These strategies work by helping you change your thought patterns and regulate your physical responses. Let's dive into a few key CBT techniques you can start using today.

Behavioral Activation: Take Action Against Anxiety

Anxiety has a sneaky way of making you avoid things— texting someone first, speaking up in class, trying out for a team, or even going to a social event. The more you avoid, the stronger the anxiety gets. That's where behavioral activation comes in!

This CBT technique helps you face your fears step by step instead of letting anxiety control your decisions. One of the best ways to do this is to schedule the activity you've been avoiding. When you put it on your calendar, it becomes a real plan—not just something to overthink and worry about.

How to Use Behavioral Activation

Follow these steps to use behavioral activation:

1. **Identify what you're avoiding:** Is there something you've been putting off because it makes you anxious? It could be sending a message in a group chat, going to a school dance, ordering food by yourself, or wearing a fun outfit you love but are scared to be judged for.

2. **Make a plan:** Instead of waiting until you "feel ready," schedule it like an appointment. Pick a specific time and date. For example:

   ○ If you're anxious about talking to a new friend, plan to message them after school.

   ○ If trying a new workout class makes you nervous, invite a friend to go with you next Saturday.

   ○ If public speaking stresses you out, practice reading out loud to yourself first before volunteering in class.

3. **Start small and build up:** Don't pressure yourself to do everything at once! Choose an easier step first and work your way up.

Here are some ways you can try to challenge avoidance and boost your confidence:

- Wear something fun, colorful, or different for a day, even if it makes you nervous. Confidence grows with practice!

- Send the text you're overthinking. Stop rereading it 20 times. Just hit send!

- Host a karaoke night, even if it's just at home! Sing your heart out, even if you think you sound terrible.

- Go to a store and ask for help. It's a great way to practice talking to people without overthinking.

- Order food by yourself. Walk up, place your order, and own it!

- Make a bucket list of "scary but exciting" things. Start crossing them off one by one!

- The more you avoid something, the heavier it can feel. But when you face your fears, even in small steps, they often start to feel more manageable over time. It's all about building that courage and trust in yourself. You're capable of handling more than you may realize.

- Confidence isn't something you're born with—it's built by doing things that scare you!

- Once you push past avoidance, you'll realize you're way stronger than your anxiety wants you to believe.

Grounding Exercises: Bring Yourself Back to the Present

Anxiety often pulls you into "what-ifs"—worrying about the future or overthinking the past. Grounding helps bring your focus back to right now, which can stop anxious thoughts from spiraling.

Try this:

1. **The 5-4-3-2-1 method**: Look around and name…

   - 5 things you can *see*

   - 4 things you can *touch*

   - 3 things you can *hear*

   - 2 things you can *smell*

   - 1 thing you can *taste*

2. **Hold onto something solid**: A cool piece of jewelry, a smooth rock, or a soft blanket can help anchor you in the moment.

3. **Engage your senses**: Run your hands under cold water, sip a warm drink, or listen to calming music to shift your focus.

Tip: If your thoughts are racing, say to yourself: *I am safe. I am in control. I am in this moment.*

Progressive Muscle Relaxation: Let Go of Tension

Stress and anxiety often show up as tension in your body—tight shoulders, clenched jaw, or a stiff neck. Progressive muscle relaxation (PMR) helps you release that tension by tensing and relaxing different muscle groups.

Here's how to practice PMR:

1. Find a quiet space and sit or lie down comfortably.

2. Start with your feet. Squeeze the muscles in your toes and hold for five seconds, then release.

3. Move up to your legs—tense your calves and thighs, hold for five seconds, then release.

4. Continue working up your body (stomach, chest, hands, arms, shoulders, neck) until you reach your face. Scrunch it up, hold, then relax.

5. Finish by taking a few deep breaths and noticing how your body feels lighter.

Tip: This is great before bed if anxiety makes it hard to sleep!

Thought Challenging: Questioning Your Thoughts Instead of Accepting Them

Thought challenging is a technique that helps you step back and look at your thoughts more objectively instead of automatically believing the worst.

What Is It?

- Instead of assuming your thoughts are 100% true, you examine the evidence from your real life.

- You learn to recognize cognitive distortions— thinking patterns that make situations seem worse than they actually are.

- You replace negative or unproductive thoughts with more balanced and realistic perspectives.

Why Does It Work?

Thought challenging is a game changer because

- anxiety often makes it hard to think rationally. Thought challenging helps you break the cycle of negative thinking and see things from a clearer perspective.

- it teaches you that just because you feel something doesn't mean it's true.

- when you challenge negative thoughts, they lose their power over you.

How to Use Thought Challenging

Follow these steps to challenge your thoughts:

1. Notice the negative thought. For example: *Everyone at the party will think I'm awkward.*

2. Ask yourself: *What's the evidence? Has this actually happened before? Do I have proof that people don't like me?*

3. Consider alternative explanations. For instance, *Maybe people are focused on their own conversations, not judging me. Maybe I'm fun to be around, and I don't even realize it.*

4. Create a more realistic and balanced thought. *I might feel awkward at first, but that doesn't mean others will notice or care. I can still have fun.*

Here is a challenge for you: Next time you have a negative thought, write it down and fact-check it like a detective. You might be surprised how often your brain exaggerates things!

Take Control: Start Challenging Your Thoughts Today

Remember, anxiety doesn't have to control you. The techniques we've discussed—whether it's thought challenging, deep breathing, or behavioral activation—are all tools to help you rewire your brain and face fear head-on. It's okay if it feels tough at first. Every small step you take is progress. You are building resilience and learning to push back against anxiety with each challenge you face.

Start by picking one of the techniques you learned in this chapter and practicing it this week. Track your progress and see how it helps you change your thinking and responses over time. You might even be surprised at how quickly you can shift your mindset and reduce your anxiety.

You've got this! The next time you feel anxiety creeping in, take a deep breath, challenge those unhelpful thoughts, and take action. You are stronger than your fears.

In the next chapter, we'll dive into mindfulness, a powerful practice that can help you stay present and manage stress even more effectively.

Chapter 4: The Power of Now (Mindfulness and Grounding Techniques)

Camille was a 17-year-old confident girl, but she worried a lot about the future. *What if she didn't get into the right college? What if she embarrassed herself in front of her classmates? What if she wasn't good enough?* Her mind was always racing, filled with "what-ifs" and worst-case scenarios. But could she learn to harness control over her emotions and find a way to calm herself? Let's find out!

One afternoon, feeling overwhelmed, Camille wandered into the forest behind her house. Usually, the quiet rustling of the leaves and the scent of pine helped her relax, but today, her thoughts were too loud. She walked quickly, her heart pounding, trying to outpace her own worries.

Then, something caught her eye—a tiny spider, spinning a web between two branches. At first, it seemed like any other spider, but as the sunlight hit the web, it shimmered with unexpected colors—blues, purples, and golds, like a rainbow woven into silk.

Camille stopped.

She crouched down, mesmerized, watching as the spider moved deliberately, pulling each thread with care. It didn't rush. It didn't hesitate. It simply focused on the task at hand, which was weaving one strand at a time.

Camille took a deep breath and watched.

Her thoughts, for once, slowed. The spider wasn't worrying about the wind that might tear its web or whether it would catch enough food. It was simply doing what was necessary, moment by moment.

A breeze passed through, shaking the delicate web. Camille tensed, expecting it to snap. But the spider didn't panic. It simply waited, still and patient, until the wind settled. Then, it continued its work, undisturbed.

Camille exhaled.

She had spent so much time worrying about the future, about things beyond her control. But right now, she was here. Right now, she could breathe. Right now, she could simply be.

She sat down on the forest floor and focused on her breath. Inhale. Exhale. Slowly, her heartbeat steadied.

For the first time all day, she wasn't lost in fear. She wasn't trying to control everything. She was just present, in the moment—just like the rainbow spider.

And maybe, just maybe, that was the secret to finding calm through mindfulness. Mindfulness helped her let go of the need to control everything; she just had to breathe, be aware, and trust that she could handle whatever came next.

Just like Camille, you can use mindfulness to ground yourself in the present. Are you ready to learn how?

What Is Mindfulness?

Mindfulness is simple. It means bringing your attention back to right now—again and again.

Mindfulness helps you tune into what's happening in the moment instead of getting lost in worries about the future or regrets about the past. One way to do this is by paying attention to your senses—what you see, hear, feel, or even smell. You can practice mindfulness while meditating and also when doing everyday things like walking, eating, or brushing your teeth.

When your mind is full, it's the opposite of mindfulness. Your thoughts jump from one thing to another—what you should've said in a conversation, whether you'll pass a test, or what someone thinks of you. The brain naturally loves to overthink and overanalyze. That's just what it does. But when it's always racing, it's easy to feel overwhelmed and stressed.

Mindfulness helps you train your brain to slow down and focus on what's in front of you. Instead of letting your thoughts pull you in a million directions, you learn to notice them without letting them take over. It's like being in control of your mind rather than letting it run wild.

At first, it might feel impossible to quiet your thoughts. But with practice, you get better at it—just like learning a new skill. And over time, something amazing happens. Your thoughts become less distracting and you start to feel calmer, more focused, and even happier.

This feeling of being fully present—without overthinking, without stress—is true mindfulness.

How Mindfulness Reduces Anxiety

Mindfulness is like having a secret tool in your back pocket, ready to help when anxiety starts creeping in.

Stops the Anxiety Spiral

Ever notice how one tiny worry can snowball into a full-blown panic? It starts with, *Did I sound weird in that text?* and suddenly, you're convinced no one likes you. Mindfulness helps you hit the pause button. Instead of getting dragged into every anxious thought, you learn to notice it, take a deep breath, and bring yourself back to now.

Lowers Stress Hormones

When you're stressed, your body releases cortisol—the hormone responsible for that tight feeling in your chest, sweaty palms, and racing heart. Mindfulness is like pressing a "chill out" switch. By focusing on your breath or your surroundings, you tell your brain, *Hey, we're safe!* and your body responds by calming down. It's science, but it also feels like magic (Hoshaw, 2022).

Improves Focus

Anxiety loves to pull your attention in a million directions. *What if I fail this test? What if I embarrass myself? What if my future is a disaster?!* Mindfulness trains your brain to stay in the moment. When your thoughts stop jumping all over the place, it's easier to concentrate on what actually matters—whether that's studying, a conversation, or just enjoying a quiet moment.

Creates Emotional Distance

Think of your anxious thoughts like pop-up ads on your phone. If you click on every single one, you'll end up overwhelmed. Mindfulness helps you see thoughts as just thoughts—not facts, not emergencies. Instead of reacting automatically, you learn to pause and decide whether a thought is even worth your time. And honestly? Most anxious thoughts are not worth the stress.

Making Space for Mindfulness

Research shows that mindfulness techniques can reduce anxiety and boost your mood. A study in 2010 found that mindfulness-based practices not only help in the moment but also create long-term benefits for mental well-being (Ackerman, 2017). That means the more you practice, the better you'll get at handling stress and anxiety when they show up.

Mental Shifts to Be More Mindful

So, how can you start using mindfulness to manage anxiety? It all begins with your mindset. Here are 10 simple mental shifts that can help you stay present, worry less, and feel more in control of your emotions:

1. Set an Intention

Before anything else, decide that you're ready to work with your anxiety instead of fighting against it. Simply recognizing that you want to feel calmer is a powerful first step.

2. See Things With a Fresh Perspective

It's easy to get stuck in the same thought patterns, but what if you looked at your worries in a new way? Keeping an open mind can help you find different solutions and feel less trapped by your thoughts.

3. Be Patient With Yourself

Change doesn't happen overnight. Some days will feel easier than others, and that's okay. Anxiety doesn't disappear instantly, but by practicing mindfulness regularly, you'll build the skills to manage it better.

4. Acknowledge Your Feelings

Instead of pushing anxiety away, try to notice it without judgment. "I feel anxious right now" is a powerful statement. It reminds you that feelings come and go—they don't define you.

5. Let Go of Self-Judgment

It's easy to think, *Why am I feeling this way?* or *I should be stronger than this.* But judging yourself for having anxiety only makes it worse. Instead, accept your emotions as they are—without criticism.

6. Don't Force Things to Change

When anxiety hits, your first instinct might be to push it away. But mindfulness teaches us to sit with discomfort instead of fighting it. The more you allow yourself to feel, the more those anxious thoughts will naturally pass.

7. Trust Yourself

You've been through tough moments before, and you got through them. Trust that you have the strength to handle your emotions, even when they feel big and overwhelming.

8. Allow Yourself to Feel

Instead of spending energy trying to block out anxiety, try to just let it be. Often, emotions lose their power when we stop running from them.

9. Be Kind to Yourself

Think about how you'd comfort a friend who's feeling anxious. Would you tell them to "just get over it"? Of course not! Treat yourself with the same kindness and understanding you'd offer someone you care about.

10. Keep Things in Perspective

No feeling lasts forever. Anxiety might feel huge in the moment, but it's only a small part of your life. By stepping back and seeing the bigger picture, you can remind yourself that this, too, shall pass.

Once you are mentally prepared, you will be able to include mindfulness in your routine. But the question remains: What are some of the best mindfulness practices?

Simple, Quick Mindfulness Exercises

Let's dive into the world of mindfulness and start by exploring some simple exercises that can help bring calm and focus to our busy lives.

Mindful Seeing: Using Your Eyes to Calm Your Mind

Your eyes take in thousands of images every day, but how often do you really *see* what's in front of you? Mindful seeing is about slowing down and truly noticing the details of the world around you. Instead of getting lost in your thoughts, you focus on colors, shapes, shadows, and movements—bringing yourself back to the present moment.

When Can You Use Mindful Seeing?

Together, let's consider some scenarios where you can put mindful seeing to use:

Scenario 1: Feeling Overwhelmed by Schoolwork

You're drowning in assignments, your to-do list is a mile long, and your brain won't stop buzzing. Instead of spiraling, step outside (or even look out a window). Pick one thing to focus on—a tree, the sky, or the way the sunlight hits your desk. Notice the colors, textures, and movement. Breathe in. Breathe out. Let your mind settle.

Scenario 2: Nervous Before a Presentation

Your heart is pounding, your palms are sweaty, and you're convinced you'll forget everything. Before stepping up, take a moment to look around. Notice the patterns on the floor, the color of the walls, or how your friend's jacket crinkles when they move. Focusing on these little details can help ground you and take the edge off your nerves.

Scenario 3: Overthinking a Social Situation

You sent a text, and now you're overanalyzing every word. *Did I sound weird? Should I have added an emoji? Why haven't they replied?!* Instead of getting caught in the "what if" loop, find something beautiful to focus on—a flower, the ripples in your drink, the way your curtains sway. Let yourself see without judgment or overthinking.

Mindful seeing is a simple trick, but it can help you feel calmer, more present, and less caught up in anxious thoughts. The world is full of tiny, beautiful details—you just have to look.

The Body Scan: Tuning Into Your Body to Calm Your Mind

Your body and mind are connected. When you're anxious, your muscles tense up, your heart beats faster, and you might not even realize you're clenching your jaw or holding your breath. A body scan is a simple mindfulness exercise that helps you check in with your body, release tension, and bring yourself back to the present.

Here is how to do a body scan:

1. **Find a quiet spot:** Sit or lie down somewhere comfortable. Close your eyes if you want, or keep them slightly open.

2. **Take several deep breaths:** Breathe in through your nose, hold briefly, and then exhale slowly through your mouth.

3. **Start at your toes:** Focus on your feet. Notice if they feel warm, cold, tingly, or relaxed. If they feel tense, imagine sending your breath there, letting them soften.

4. **Move up your body:** Shift your attention to your legs, stomach, arms, shoulders, neck, and finally your head. With each area, notice any tightness and relax it as you exhale.

5. **If your mind wanders, that's okay:** Just gently bring your focus back to your body.

6. **End with a deep breath:** After scanning your whole body, take one last deep breath and slowly open your eyes.

When to Use the Body Scan

Let's look at some situations where you can use a body scan exercise:

Scenario 1: Struggling to Fall Asleep

Your mind won't stop replaying the day, and you're tossing and turning. Instead of fighting it, do a body scan. Focusing on relaxing each part of your body helps shift your mind away from overthinking and into rest mode.

Scenario 2: Feeling Nervous Before an Event

Whether it's a big test, a performance, or a social event, nerves can make your body feel shaky and tense. A quick body scan can help you release that tension, making you feel more in control and confident.

Scenario 3: Stressing Out While Studying

You've been hunched over your desk for hours, and your neck and shoulders are tight. Pausing for a quick body scan helps you check in, stretch out, and reset before diving back in with a clearer head.

The body scan is an easy way to listen to your body and give it what it needs. Try it out, and you might be surprised at how much calmer you feel!

Breathing Techniques: Simple Ways to Calm Anxiety in Minutes

Your breath is one of the most powerful tools you have to calm your mind and body. When you're anxious, your breathing becomes shallow and quick, which makes you feel even more on edge. By slowing and controlling your breath, you can signal to your brain that everything is fine.

These simple breathing techniques take just a few minutes and can help you feel more grounded and in control.

The 4-7-8 Breath (Deep Relaxation)

The 4-7-8 breath technique slows the heart rate, activates the relaxation response, and helps ease stress. It's perfect for when you feel tense or need to unwind before bed.

Here is how you can do it:

1. Breathe in deeply through your nose for 4 seconds.

2. Hold your breath for 7 seconds.

3. Repeat for a few rounds, focusing on the rhythm of your breath.

4. Exhale slowly through your mouth for 8 seconds (like you're blowing out a candle).

The 4-7-8 breath technique is best for calming nerves before a test, relaxing after a stressful day, or winding down before sleep.

Box Breathing (Regaining Control in Stressful Moments)

Athletes, performers, and even Navy SEALs often use box breathing to stay calm under pressure. It helps regulate your breathing, clear your mind, and regain control when feeling overwhelmed.

Let's try it together right now. Ready?

1. Breathe in deeply through your nose for 4 seconds.

2. Hold your breath for 4 seconds.

3. Exhale slowly through your mouth for 4 seconds.

4. Hold your breath for 4 seconds before starting again.

Box breathing is best in moments of panic, before a big presentation, or when your mind is racing.

Breathe Like You're Blowing a Dandelion (Gentle Anxiety Relief)

Breathing like you are blowing a dandelion helps shift your focus away from anxious thoughts by giving you a calming visual element to focus on. It also naturally slows your breath, helping you feel more relaxed.

To practice this, follow these steps:

1. Imagine a dandelion puff in front of you.

2. Take a slow, deep breath in through your nose.

3. Exhale softly and steadily through your mouth, like you're blowing the seeds off a dandelion.

4. Repeat, imagining each exhale carrying your worries away.

Breathing like blowing a dandelion is ideal for easing social anxiety, calming pre-test jitters, or anytime you feel overwhelmed.

Tip: Try these techniques whenever you feel anxious, and see which one works best for you. With practice, they'll become second nature and help you stay calm and centered, no matter what comes your way.

Visualization Exercises

Visualization exercises are another powerful tool in your mindfulness toolkit. When anxiety hits hard, creating a mental safe space to escape to can be incredibly comforting. Visualization is a mindfulness technique that helps you shift your focus away from anxious thoughts and into a space of peace and security.

Building Your Personal Safe Space

To build your personal safe space, close your eyes for a moment and take a deep breath in. Now, imagine yourself in a place where you feel completely at ease. It could be anything:

- a tropical beach with the warm sand beneath your toes, the gentle sound of waves crashing, and the salty breeze on your skin

- a peaceful forest with the rustling of leaves, the scent of pine, and the dappled sunlight streaming through the trees

- a cozy bedroom with a warm blanket wrapped around you, the soft glow of fairy lights, and your favorite book in your lap

- a fun memory with a place you've been that made you happy, like a carnival with twinkling lights or a childhood playground

Take your time and add as much detail as possible. What colors do you see? What sounds fill the space? Are there any scents in the air? The more vivid you make your visualization, the more effective it will be at pulling you away from stress and into relaxation.

Tip: If you struggle to create a mental image, look at photos of places that inspire peace, like beaches, gardens, or quiet cafés. With time, your brain will remember these details, making your visualization even stronger.

Whenever the outside world feels overwhelming, you can retreat to this personal sanctuary. The best part? No one can take it away from you. It's always there, waiting for you whenever you need it.

Letting Go of Anxiety

Anxiety loves to trick you into thinking that your thoughts are facts. But here's the truth: Thoughts are just thoughts. They don't define you, and you don't have to let them control you.

To practice floating thoughts, try this:

1. **Imagine your mind as a clear blue sky.** Your thoughts are like soft, white clouds floating by. Some are big; some are small. Some move quickly; others take their time.

2. **Now, watch as your anxious thoughts appear as clouds.** Maybe one says, *What if I fail my test?* or *I don't think they like me.* Instead of engaging with these thoughts, simply notice them. Acknowledge their presence without reacting.

3. **Gently let the cloud drift away.** Much like real clouds, these thoughts don't last forever. They come and they go. You don't have to chase after them or try to stop them. They're just passing by.

4. **Return your focus to the sky.** No matter how many clouds appear, the blue sky is always there—calm, steady, and unchanged. The sky represents you, and the clouds are just temporary thoughts.

This exercise helps you create distance between yourself and your worries. Instead of getting stuck in anxious thinking, you learn to observe your thoughts and let them go. The more you practice, the easier it becomes to release negative thoughts before they take over.

Visualization is like building a mental superpower—it trains your brain to create calm even in stressful moments. With practice, it becomes easier to step away from anxious thoughts and into a space of peace and control.

Next time your mind feels chaotic, remember: You have the power to escape to a place of calm. Whether it's a quiet beach, a childhood memory, or a blue sky full of floating clouds, your mental sanctuary is always just a breath away.

Staying Present, Staying Strong

Mindfulness won't make anxiety disappear forever, but it will give you the tools to handle it with more confidence and less fear. The more you practice, the simpler it gets. So the next time anxiety creeps in, take a breath, bring yourself back to the moment, and remind yourself: *I've got this.*

Up next is handling panic attacks like a pro—because when panic hits, knowing what to do can make all the difference.

Chapter 5: Handling Panic Attacks Like a Pro

Being a teenager is not easy. It comes with a lot of pressure—school, friendships, family expectations, and figuring out who you are. Sometimes, it can all feel overwhelming.

This is what Amelia was struggling with as well. It started in the middle of lunch when she overheard a group of girls whispering and laughing while looking at their phones. A sinking feeling settled in her stomach. She just knew it was about her.

Then her phone buzzed. A new post.

Her fingers trembled as she opened it—and there it was. A photo of her, taken from a weird angle while she was eating, mid-bite, looking completely ridiculous. The caption? "Bon appétit, loser." The comments were already piling up. "Omg I can't unsee this." "Why does she eat like that??" "Someone get her a lesson on how to be normal."

Her chest tightened. Her heart pounded so fast it felt like it might burst. The cafeteria noise faded into the background, replaced by the deafening rush of panic in her ears. Her hands felt numb, her breathing turned shallow, and suddenly, she couldn't get enough air. Was she sick? What was happening?

She grabbed her bag and rushed out, barely making it to an empty classroom before her legs gave out. She slid to the floor, gripping her knees, trying to stop the shaking.

It wasn't until later that Amelia learned what had happened—she had experienced her first panic attack. And while it felt terrifying in the moment, she soon discovered that panic attacks don't have to control her life.

If you've ever felt something similar, you're not alone. In this chapter, we'll talk about what panic attacks are, why they happen, and, most importantly, how you can handle them like a pro.

What Is a Panic Attack?

I know what you're thinking: *Didn't we already talk about panic attacks in Chapter 2?* Yes—but this time, we're diving deeper. Let's break it down even further so you can understand exactly what's happening and how to take control when panic strikes.

A panic attack is an intense surge of fear or discomfort that comes on suddenly and reaches its peak within minutes. While the experience can feel overwhelming and even terrifying, it's important to remember that panic attacks, though distressing, are not dangerous.

What Happens in Your Body During a Panic Attack?

Panic attacks trigger the body's fight-or-flight response, which is designed to protect you from danger. The problem here is that your brain perceives a threat that isn't actually there, setting off a chain reaction of physical symptoms, including:

- **Rapid heartbeat (palpitations):** Your heart starts pounding because your body thinks it needs to pump extra blood to your muscles to prepare for action.

- **Shortness of breath or hyperventilation:** You may feel like you can't get enough air, but in reality, you're breathing too fast, which lowers carbon dioxide levels and makes you feel lightheaded.

- **Dizziness or feeling faint:** Changes in blood flow and breathing patterns can make you feel like you're going to pass out, even though you won't.

- **Chest pain or tightness:** The combination of muscle tension and increased heart rate can create a squeezing or aching sensation in your chest. Many people mistake this for a heart attack.

- **Tingling or numbness:** Blood is being redirected to essential organs, which can make your fingers, hands, or face feel tingly or numb.

- **Sweating or chills:** Your body is preparing to cool itself down as part of the stress response.

- **A sense of doom or detachment:** Many people feel like something terrible is about to happen or experience a surreal, "out-of-body" sensation.

Panic attacks can be frightening and overwhelming, like a sudden storm that arrives out of nowhere. It isn't just in your head—it's happening in your body, and knowing this helps us realize we're not alone or imagining things.

What Increases Your Risk of Panic Disorder?

Certain factors can increase the likelihood of developing panic disorder. These include the following:

Family History

Panic disorder often runs in families. If a first-degree relative—like a parent, sibling, or child—has been diagnosed with the condition, you may have up to a 40% greater likelihood of experiencing panic attacks (*Panic Attacks*, n.d.). This indicates that genetic factors can significantly contribute to the development of panic disorder.

Other Mental Health Conditions

Having a history of other mental health conditions, especially anxiety disorders or depression, can make someone more prone to panic attacks. The presence of these conditions can heighten emotional sensitivity and contribute to the physical and emotional triggers that lead to panic.

Adverse Childhood Experiences (ACEs)

Adverse childhood experiences (ACEs) refer to negative or traumatic events that occur before the age of 18. These can include things like abuse, neglect, the loss of a parent, or witnessing violence. Studies have shown that individuals who experience ACEs are at an increased risk for developing a variety of mental health conditions, including panic attacks and panic disorder (*Panic Attacks*, n.d.). The long-lasting effects of these experiences can make the body and mind more vulnerable to stress, leading to heightened anxiety responses.

What Triggers Panic Attacks?

Panic attacks can occur with or without a specific trigger, which can make them especially unsettling. However, there are certain situations and experiences that are more likely to bring on a panic attack for some individuals.

No Clear Trigger

For many individuals with panic disorder, the attacks occur without any apparent trigger. One of the hallmarks of panic disorder is that the panic attacks occur unexpectedly, often without any obvious external stressor. This unpredictability can create an ongoing sense of fear as individuals begin to worry about when the next attack might happen.

Phobias and Specific Triggers

While panic attacks can happen without warning, some individuals may experience attacks related to specific fears. For example, someone with trypanophobia (fear of needles) might have a panic attack if they need to get a blood test. Similarly, individuals with a fear of flying may experience panic when boarding a plane.

Fear of Having a Panic Attack

For some people, the mere thought of having a panic attack is enough to trigger one. This is because the body's physical reaction to anxiety—such as a rapid heartbeat or shortness of breath—can be misinterpreted as the beginning of a panic attack. This leads to a vicious cycle: the fear of an attack causes the body to react as if one is happening, which in turn increases anxiety and can trigger an actual panic attack.

Did you know? The difference between an anxiety attack and a panic attack is significant, even though they may feel similar. Anxiety attacks are usually triggered by a specific stressor or worry, like an upcoming test or a difficult conversation. They build gradually, with symptoms like tension, restlessness, and a sense of unease.

Panic attacks, on the other hand, come on suddenly and without warning, often without any clear trigger. They reach their peak within minutes and involve intense physical symptoms like rapid heartbeat, shortness of breath, and dizziness.

While both can be distressing, panic attacks are typically much more intense and are associated with the fight-or-flight response. In contrast, anxiety attacks tend to be more related to ongoing stress or worry.

Can You Stop a Panic Attack?

Absolutely, yes! While panic attacks can feel uncontrollable and overwhelming, there are proven techniques to help you regain control and stop them in their tracks. Let's create a three-step panic attack rescue plan together.

Step 1: Remember That It Will Pass

When a panic attack begins, it can feel all-encompassing, as though the intense emotions and physical sensations will never end. However, the most important thing to remember in that moment is that this feeling is temporary. Panic attacks, while frightening, don't last forever. The symptoms you're experiencing—racing heart, shortness of breath, dizziness—are all part of the body's natural fight-or-flight response, but they won't harm you.

Remind yourself that this is a moment of heightened anxiety, and like all moments, it will eventually pass. Acknowledge that it may feel overwhelming now, but you're not in danger. Panic attacks typically reach their peak intensity within 10 minutes, after which the symptoms start to subside (Smith, 2023). Knowing this can provide a sense of relief, as you can trust that the discomfort will lessen with time. Reassure yourself that the feeling of panic is temporary and that you will soon feel like yourself again.

This step is about grounding yourself in the knowledge that panic attacks are brief episodes, not life-threatening events. By accepting the temporary nature of these feelings, you give yourself the emotional space to begin calming your body and mind.

Affirmations to Calm Your Mind

In the midst of a panic attack, it can be easy to get lost in the fear and intensity of the moment. Affirmations can help ground you, shift your focus, and remind you that this, too, shall pass. Here are some statements you can tell yourself to help regain control and calm your mind:

- **"This feeling will pass. I am safe."** Remind yourself that panic is temporary and that you're in no immediate danger. This simple affirmation can help quiet the mind and create space for calming thoughts.

- **"I am in control of my breathing."** Focus on your breath, and remind yourself that you have the power to slow it down. Breathing deeply can trigger the body's natural relaxation response.

- **"This is just anxiety, and it can't harm me."** Reassure yourself that anxiety, while uncomfortable, won't cause any long-term harm. It's simply a physical and emotional reaction to stress.

- **"I am strong, and I can handle this."** Remind yourself of your inner strength and resilience. You've faced challenges before, and you can get through this one, too.

- **"My body is reacting, but I am not in danger."** Recognizing that the body's response is just a reaction to stress can help separate the feelings from a sense of imminent threat.

- **"I am grounded in the present moment."** Focus on the now and try to let go of worries about the past or future. This affirmation brings your attention back to what you can control.

- **"I trust that I will feel better soon."** Trusting in the process and knowing that the panic attack will subside helps create a sense of hope during the most intense moments.

You can repeat these affirmations aloud, in your mind, or even write them down if it helps. The key is to use language that reassures and comforts you, reminding yourself that panic attacks, though unsettling, are not permanent and will not cause lasting harm.

Step 2: Take Deep Breaths

When panic strikes, your body often responds with rapid, shallow breathing, which can make you feel even more dizzy or lightheaded. One of the most effective ways to counteract this is by focusing on taking deep, steady breaths. Deep breathing helps slow your heart rate, bring oxygen back into balance, and send a calming signal to your nervous system.

To practice deep breathing, follow these steps:

1. Find a quiet place where you can relax. Sit comfortably with your back straight, or lie down if that's more comfortable.

2. Close your eyes to minimize distractions and focus on your breath. Slowly inhale through your nose, which will fill your lungs with air.

3. Breathe in deeply through your nose for 4 seconds, feeling your belly expand as your lungs fill.

4. Exhale slowly through your mouth for 6 seconds, and let all the air leave your lungs. Try to make your exhale longer than your inhale to promote relaxation.

5. Repeat this pattern for 2–3 minutes, concentrating on the sensation of your breath. You can count quietly or out loud to help you keep track of your breathing.

You can also pick your favorite breathing technique from the previous chapter and keep repeating it for some time.

Alternative Method: Rebalancing Your Oxygen

If you're still feeling lightheaded, another technique is to cup your hands over your nose and mouth. By breathing into your hands, you reintroduce a stable flow of oxygen and carbon dioxide, helping to calm your system and reduce dizziness. This can be especially useful if hyperventilation has caused you to feel unbalanced.

Taking deep, mindful breaths helps slow down your nervous system, bringing you back to the present moment and helping you regain control.

Step 3: Engage Your Senses (Grounding Techniques)

Physical sensations can be incredibly grounding. Try holding something cold, like an ice pack, a frozen water bottle, or a cold drink, against your skin. The sharp contrast in temperature stimulates your nervous system, breaking the cycle of panic and bringing you back to the present. If cold isn't comforting, try warmth instead—wrap yourself in a soft blanket, hold a warm mug of tea, or take a warm shower to relax tense muscles.

You can also incorporate some movement to get yourself out of the panic attack.

When anxiety hits, your body releases adrenaline, preparing you to either fight or flee. Since you don't need to escape from danger, moving your body can help use up that excess energy and bring your system back to balance. Try any of the following:

- Take a short walk (even around the room).

- Shake out your arms or legs to release tension.

- Stretch your muscles, focusing on areas where you feel tightness.

- Do light jumping or stomp your feet to feel connected to the ground.

Sound also helps you tune into reality. Listen closely to the sounds around you—a ticking clock, birds outside, or music.

If you have a calming playlist, put on a favorite song and focus on the lyrics or melody. Some people find white noise, nature sounds, or ASMR helpful in calming the mind.

Scent is strongly connected to memory and emotions. Smelling a familiar scent, like lavender, peppermint, or your favorite lotion, can provide comfort and familiarity (Smith, 2023). If you have access to food or drink, try sipping a strong-flavored tea, sucking on a mint, or chewing gum. The taste and texture can help pull you out of panic and back into the present.

Try experimenting with different methods to find what works best for you—having a go-to grounding strategy can make a huge difference when anxiety strikes.

Long-Term Strategies for Reducing Panic Attack Frequency and Intensity

While immediate techniques can help stop a panic attack in the moment, long-term strategies can reduce their frequency and intensity over time. By understanding triggers, making lifestyle changes, and building emotional resilience, you can regain a sense of control and lessen the impact of panic attacks.

Identify and Manage Triggers

Understanding what sets off your panic attacks is the first step in preventing them. Keep a journal to track when and where they occur, what you were doing beforehand, and any thoughts or feelings that arose. Common triggers include:

- stress and anxiety buildup

- caffeine or stimulants

- lack of sleep

- certain environments or social situations

- negative thought patterns

Once you identify your triggers, you can take proactive steps to manage them, such as reducing caffeine intake, improving sleep habits, or addressing underlying stressors.

Practice Regular Relaxation Techniques

Training your body and mind to stay calm can help prevent panic attacks from escalating. Incorporate relaxation practices into your daily routine, such as:

- deep breathing exercises

- progressive muscle relaxation

- meditation and mindfulness

- visualization

These techniques help regulate your nervous system, making it easier to stay grounded during moments of anxiety.

Maintain a Healthy Lifestyle

Your physical health has a direct impact on your emotional well-being. When your body is well-nourished, rested, and active, you're better equipped to handle stress and anxiety, reducing the likelihood of panic attacks. Incorporating healthy habits into your daily routine can help regulate your nervous system, balance mood-stabilizing chemicals, and build resilience against panic triggers.

Lack of sleep increases vulnerability to stress, anxiety, and panic attacks. When you're sleep-deprived, your brain becomes more reactive to perceived threats and intensifies feelings of fear and anxiety. Research suggests that teenage girls need 8–10 hours of sleep per night, yet most only get 6.5–7.5 hours due to late bedtimes and early school starts (*Teenagers and Sleep*, 2018). This natural shift in a teen's body clock makes it harder to fall asleep early, but maintaining good sleep habits can help.

Can we change school start times? Nope, not likely. But can we go to bed earlier? Absolutely, yes. Is it fun? Not really. But is it worth it? Totally.

Since schools aren't handing out permission slips for extra sleep, the best move is to outsmart the system. Try setting a "fake bedtime" 30 minutes earlier than you actually need to sleep—because let's be honest, there will be at least one more scroll, text, or random deep thought about life before you actually doze off.

Let's explore some additional tips to improve your sleep quality:

- **Maintain a consistent schedule:** Try to go to bed and wake up at the same time every day, including weekends, to help regulate your body's internal clock.

- **Limit screen time before bed:** Blue light from phones and computers can disrupt melatonin production, which makes it harder to fall asleep. Try reading a book or listening to calming music instead.

- **Create a relaxing bedtime routine:** Wind down with a warm bath, light stretching, or deep breathing to signal to your body that it's time to rest.

- **Work on your sleep environment:** Make sure your room is cool, dark, and quiet. Consider using blackout curtains and white noise machines if necessary.

Getting enough quality sleep helps regulate mood, lowers anxiety, and reduces the likelihood of panic attacks. Making small adjustments to your sleep routine can have a big impact on your emotional well-being.

Build a Strong Support System

Having people you trust can make a huge difference when dealing with panic attacks. But let's be real—asking for support can feel awkward for some. Let me tell you, you don't need a whole speech prepared. Here's how to build a support system that actually helps:

Identify Your Go-To People

Think about who makes you feel safe and understood. This could be:

- a best friend who always hypes you up

- a family member who listens without judgment

- a teacher, coach, or school counselor who genuinely cares

- a therapist (because professionals exist for a reason!)

Not everyone needs to know everything. Some friends might be great for distractions and fun, while others are better for deep talks.

Have "The Talk," But Be Casual

You don't have to sit someone down with a dramatic "We need to talk" moment. Instead, try something like:

"Hey, just so you know, I sometimes get panic attacks. If that ever happens around you, just remind me to breathe and that it'll pass."

Or "I've been dealing with anxiety lately. Can I text you if I ever need a little support?"

Most people want to help but don't know how unless you tell them!

Create a "Crisis Plan" Together

Pick a code word or emoji you can send when you need support but don't want to explain everything. You and your person can agree on simple ways they can help, like:

- sending a funny meme or distraction

- talking about anything *but* panic

- reminding you that you're safe and that this will pass

Set Boundaries

Support is great, but you don't have to overshare or feel obligated to tell everyone everything. If someone isn't helpful or makes you feel worse, they don't need to be in your support system. Stick with the people who make you feel safe.

Be a Good Friend

Support goes both ways! Check in on your friends, listen when they need it, and make sure they know they can count on you, too. It's not about fixing each other—it's about having each other's backs.

Exposure Therapy for Panic Triggers

Avoiding situations that trigger panic attacks might feel like a quick fix, but it can make anxiety worse in the long run. Over time, avoiding triggers reinforces the belief that they are dangerous, which increases fear and anxiety. Exposure therapy is a proven technique that helps break this cycle by gradually and safely confronting triggers.

What Is Exposure Therapy?

Exposure therapy is a type of CBT in which you slowly confront situations or objects that trigger your anxiety in a safe and controlled environment. By repeatedly facing these triggers, your brain learns that they are not as frightening or dangerous as it once believed. This process can help reduce the intensity of panic attacks and the anxiety associated with them.

Steps to start exposure therapy on your own include the following:

Identifying Your Triggers

Before starting, make a list of things that typically trigger your panic attacks. These could be things such as crowded places, public speaking, certain social situations, being away from home, driving, or being in elevators. This helps you understand what situations cause the most stress, and you can work through them one step at a time.

Starting Small

Exposure therapy works best when you take small, manageable steps. If a certain situation makes you feel very anxious (like speaking in front of a group), start by practicing in smaller, lower-pressure settings:

1.   Talk to one friend or family member.

2. Practice in front of a mirror.

3. Record yourself talking, and listen to the recording.

4. Move up to a small group of trusted people.

5. Gradually work your way up to larger audiences.

Start with the situations that cause you the least amount of anxiety and work your way up. This method, called the "hierarchy of fear", lets you build confidence as you slowly face your fears.

Focusing on Relaxation Techniques During Exposure

As you expose yourself to your triggers, it's important to practice relaxation techniques (like deep breathing or grounding) to keep your body calm. For example, before entering a crowded place, you could do some deep breathing or practice mindfulness to stay grounded. This helps your body learn how to stay calm in these situations over time.

Gradually Increasing the Challenge

As you grow more comfortable with each small step, you can start to increase the intensity of your exposure. This could mean increasing the amount of time you spend in a triggering situation or making the situation a bit more challenging each time. It's essential to take these steps at your own pace and not push yourself too quickly. Overloading yourself with too much exposure too fast can backfire and increase anxiety.

Track Your Progress

Keep track of how you're feeling after each exposure. Rate your anxiety before and after the experience on a scale of 1–10 to measure progress. Over time, you'll likely notice that the anxiety diminishes with each exposure. Remember to celebrate small victories!

When to Seek Professional Help

Exposure therapy can be very effective, but it's not always easy to do alone, especially with more severe triggers. If you're struggling or feel overwhelmed, it's helpful to work with a therapist who can guide you through the process and provide support. They can help you create a personalized exposure plan and teach you additional coping skills to manage anxiety.

Know that exposure therapy is about gradual progress, not perfection. It's about learning to face fear at your own pace and understanding that panic attacks, no matter how intense, do not define you.

How to Help Someone Experiencing a Panic Attack

If someone you care about is having a panic attack, your presence and calm support can make all the difference. Here's how you can effectively help:

Stay With Them and Keep Calm

Panic attacks can feel overwhelming, both for the person experiencing them and for those around them. It's crucial to remain calm and composed. Your steady presence can provide comfort and reassurance, helping them feel less alone in their distress. Even if they're visibly shaken, your calm energy can help ground them.

Ask What They Need

Everyone experiences panic attacks differently, so it's important to ask how you can help. Some people might want space, while others might prefer you to stay close. Be gentle in your approach, and let them guide you on what feels best for them. You could say, "How can I help right now?" or "What would make you feel better?"

Speak in Simple, Soothing Sentences

During a panic attack, someone's mind is racing, and they may find it hard to process complex information. Keep your communication short, clear, and calm. Speak in a gentle, soothing tone, and avoid overwhelming them with too much information. Simple phrases like "You're okay," "I'm here with you," or "You're safe" can be very comforting.

Encourage Them to Focus on the Present

Panic attacks can make the person feel like they're spiraling out of control. Gently encourage them to focus on their surroundings and the present moment. You could help by asking them to describe something they can see, hear, or touch. For example, "Can you tell me three things you see around you right now?" or "Let's take a look at the colors of the room." This can help shift their focus away from the overwhelming sensations they're feeling.

Help Them Practice Deep Breathing

Breathing exercises can be incredibly effective in helping to slow down the body's fight-or-flight response. Guide them to breathe slowly and deeply by counting to five on each inhale and exhale. You could say, "Let's breathe together. Inhale slowly for a count of five... now exhale slowly for a count of five." Repeat this process a few times, encouraging a rhythmic pattern of breath.

Be Patient and Non-Judgmental

Sometimes, the best thing you can do is simply be patient and non-judgmental. Let them know that it's okay to feel anxious and that there's no need to apologize for having a panic attack. Sometimes, just your quiet, non-judgmental support can help them feel more secure and accepted during a difficult time.

Avoid Physical Touch (Unless They Request It)

Physical touch can be soothing for some people, but for others, it may feel overwhelming or invasive during a panic attack. Ask if they would like you to hold their hand or offer a comforting touch. If they prefer not to be touched, respect their boundaries and find other ways to comfort them.

Offer Support After the Attack

Once the panic attack starts to subside, offer support and care. They may feel exhausted, disoriented, or embarrassed. Gently check in with them and offer reassurance that it's okay to take things slow. Remind them that they are strong for having faced the experience and that they can handle future attacks as well. Ask if they need anything—whether that's water, a quiet space, or simply someone to talk to.

You've Got This!

Panic attacks can be overwhelming, but with the right tools, they don't have to take control of your life. By practicing grounding techniques and breathing exercises and making lifestyle changes, you can reduce the intensity and frequency of panic attacks. Remember, you're not alone in this journey—taking small steps every day will empower you to face challenges head-on. And now that you've got a plan for panic, get ready to take on the next chapter, which is all about social anxiety. It's time to break free from the worry of social situations and embrace the confidence that's already inside you!

Chapter 6: Conquering Social Anxiety— How to Feel Comfortable in Any Crowd

If I spill a little secret, can you promise not to tell anyone— like, not even your pet goldfish? I'm about to kick off this chapter with something personal, and I'm counting on you to be my trusted vault of secrets!

For as long as I can remember, social situations have been a constant source of anxiety for me. It started around eighth grade, and ever since, it felt like my brain was stuck on high alert. Every interaction, every conversation, even just walking into a room full of people—it all felt overwhelming to me. The embarrassment, the fear of judgment, the way my face would turn red at the worst possible moments—everything added to my social anxiety.

At one point, I even stopped wearing red because every time I did, people would point out how my shirt matched my face when I blushed. It was like a walking mood ring. I craved approval just to quiet my own self-doubt, but no matter how hard I tried to blend in or become a human camouflage, the anxiety just wouldn't take the hint and leave.

I saw a few therapists, but none of them specialized in social anxiety. The focus was often on exploring my past, searching for something that might have triggered my anxiety. I kept hoping for clarity, but instead, I ended up feeling more stuck. One of the toughest moments came when a psychiatrist reassured me that my anxiety was simply a part of life, something everyone experiences to some degree. But I knew what I was feeling went far beyond ordinary nervousness. This wasn't just shyness or overthinking.

It didn't feel normal to panic over the thought of being called on in class. Or to spend the night before school replaying worst-case scenarios in my head. Or to feel a wave of dread every time I had to walk into a crowded cafeteria. Even being around my closest friends didn't completely erase the constant, nagging self-consciousness.

At some point, I realized that the worst thing wasn't what other people thought about me—it was what I thought about myself.

I started researching social anxiety on my own and found stories from people who felt exactly the same way. For the first time, I realized I wasn't alone. Eventually, I came across something that changed everything: role-playing. Unlike traditional therapy, which focused on my past, role-playing helped me practice real-life scenarios and build confidence by stepping outside of my comfort zone.

At first, I was skeptical, but I decided to give it a try. I worked through different scenarios with a friend and practiced what I would say or do in situations that made me anxious. Slowly, I started learning ways to manage my anxiety—things like challenging my inner critic, practicing exposure in small steps, and using calming techniques in moments of panic. Role-playing allowed me to rehearse these moments and feel more prepared when they actually happened.

I won't lie and say I'm 100% anxiety-free now. I still have moments where my brain tries to pull me back into old patterns of fear and doubt. But now, I have the tools to stop the spiral before it takes over. I've also learned that self-care—things like exercise, eating well, and making time for my hobbies—makes a huge difference in my anxiety levels.

Most importantly, I've stopped fighting against myself. I don't have to be perfect, and I don't have to hide. And even though my negative thoughts still creep in sometimes, I know how to deal with them instead of letting them control me.

So, if you're reading or listening to this and feeling stuck—like social anxiety is running your life—I promise, it doesn't have to be this way forever. The first step is deciding that you deserve help. And you do.

Conquering Social Anxiety—How to Feel Comfortable in Any Crowd

Social anxiety is more than feeling nervous before a big test or having a shy moment when you're meeting new people. It's a persistent fear of being judged or negatively evaluated in social situations, and it can affect everything from how you speak in class to how you feel when you're hanging out with friends.

For many teen girls, social anxiety can show up in different ways. It might feel like your heart races or your palms sweat when you're asked to speak in front of the class, even if it's something as simple as answering a question. You might avoid school dances or social events because the thought of being around a group of people makes you anxious, or you might feel uncomfortable texting someone first for fear of saying the wrong thing. This anxiety can make everyday activities, like lunch with friends or group projects, seem overwhelming.

The good news is that social anxiety is something you can manage and even overcome. Understanding how it works in your mind and body is the first step toward feeling more comfortable in social settings.

Recognizing the Difference Between Shyness and Social Anxiety

It's important to know the difference between shyness and social anxiety because they can feel similar but are actually quite different. Shyness is a feeling of discomfort in social situations, but it doesn't usually interfere with your everyday life. For example, you might feel a little awkward when meeting new people, but once you get to know them, it passes.

Social anxiety, on the other hand, is more intense and can last for a long time. It's not just about feeling nervous—it's about fearing judgment or embarrassment to the point where it can stop you from doing things you want to do. For example, maybe you get invited to a group hangout, but the idea of meeting up with others makes you feel so anxious that you cancel at the last minute. Or maybe you avoid posting pictures or sharing your thoughts online because you're terrified of how others will react.

Here's a way to think about it: If you're shy, you might feel nervous talking to someone new, but if you have social anxiety, you might be so overwhelmed with fear about saying the wrong thing that you don't even want to talk to anyone at all.

Let's discuss a few examples to differentiate between shyness and social anxiety.

Nora is going to a party where she doesn't know most of the people. She feels a little nervous as she walks in, but once she starts talking to someone and gets to know them, she feels more comfortable. She might keep to herself a bit at first, but after a while, she's able to join in on conversations and even have some laughs with others.

Anna is invited to the same party, but the thought of walking into a room full of unfamiliar faces makes her heart race. She's consumed with the fear that others will judge her, and she starts to worry about saying the wrong thing. As soon as she walks in, she feels like everyone is staring at her, and even though she wants to attend, she might end up texting a friend to come pick her up early because she feels overwhelmed by her anxiety.

Which one of the two do you think has social anxiety?

Similarly, Sarah is in a classroom where the teacher asks for volunteers to answer a question. She feels nervous about speaking in front of everyone but decides to raise her hand anyway. She stumbles over her words a bit, but it's not as bad as she expected, and she moves on with her day.

Lily is in the same class, but the idea of being called on in front of the class makes her stomach churn. She anticipates all the possible ways she could mess up, and her mind races with thoughts like, "What if I say something dumb and everyone laughs?" When the teacher calls on her, her voice shakes, and she's unable to think clearly. Afterward, she spends hours replaying the moment in her mind, convinced that everyone is still talking about how awkward she was.

Sarah or Lily: Who is shy and who has social anxiety?

The Power of Small Mindset Shifts to Change How You Feel in Social Situations

Sometimes, the biggest barrier to conquering social anxiety isn't the situations themselves—it's the way we think about them. Our thoughts can either make us feel more anxious or help us feel more at ease. By making small mindset shifts, you can start to feel more comfortable in social situations. Here are some examples:

Challenge Your Thoughts

When you're anxious about talking to someone, your brain might tell you things like, *They'll think I'm weird*, or *I'll mess this up, and everyone will laugh at me*. These thoughts create unnecessary pressure. Instead, ask yourself, *Is this really the truth? What's the worst that could happen?* You might find that the worst-case scenario isn't nearly as bad as your mind initially led you to believe.

For example, if you're worried about talking to a group at lunch, remind yourself that they're just like you, and chances are, they're not focusing on you as much as you think. Most people are too busy worrying about themselves to judge you harshly.

Shift From *What Will They Think of Me?* to *What Can I Learn?*

One of the biggest challenges of social anxiety is the fear of being judged by others. Instead of worrying about what they might think, try to shift your focus to what you can learn from the situation. Whether you're talking to a classmate or joining a group project, you have an opportunity to grow, connect, and improve your social skills. Imagine this as a chance to practice, not a high-stakes exam.

For instance, instead of stressing about the possibility of saying something awkward in a group conversation, think of it as a way to become more comfortable with small talk and make a new connection.

Reframe Social Situations as Opportunities, Not Threats

When you have social anxiety, it's easy to see social events— like school dances or group outings—as threatening or intimidating. But by changing how you look at these situations, you can take away some of their power. For example, when you're invited to a party, instead of thinking, *I'll never fit in* or *Everyone will notice how awkward I am*, try thinking, "This is a chance to meet new people and have fun." You don't have to be perfect or have everything figured out—just being there is an accomplishment. Remember, everyone at that party has their own insecurities, too.

Focus on Listening, Not Performing

One of the reasons social anxiety feels so overwhelming is the fear of "performing" in social situations—like always having to say something smart, funny, or interesting. But the truth is, people love being listened to more than they care about what you say.

If you find yourself nervous during a conversation, instead of thinking you need to be the center of attention, try focusing on the other person. Ask questions, show interest, and listen actively. When you make someone else feel heard, you'll find the conversation flows more naturally and you can relax more.

By practicing these mindset shifts, you can begin to reframe social situations and reduce the anxiety you feel. The key is to start small, take it one step at a time, and remember that the more you practice, the more comfortable you'll become. It's not about eliminating anxiety entirely—it's about learning how to manage it so you can show up as your authentic self, no matter the crowd.

Overcoming the Fear of Judgment

The fear of being judged can be so overwhelming that it holds us back from pursuing what we truly want. It stops us from stepping outside our comfort zone, trying new things, or making unconventional choices. Too often, we ask ourselves: *What will people think? Will they approve? Am I letting them down?* These questions become barriers, preventing us from living authentically.

Stepping beyond our comfort zone can feel terrifying—but does staying within it bring you true satisfaction? If you're honest with yourself, you'll realize that avoiding judgment often comes at the cost of suppressing your true desires. When you ignore that inner voice urging you toward growth, your mind and body respond. Anxiety, frustration, and even physical symptoms may manifest as signs that you are going against your own aspirations.

Understanding the Root of Judgment Anxiety

The first step in overcoming this fear is self-awareness. When judgment makes you uncomfortable, take a moment to pause and reflect: *Why does this affect me? What emotion am I feeling— fear, sadness, anger? What am I really afraid of? Why do I seek their approval?*

When you learn to stay connected with yourself, the answers become clearer. The more honest you are with yourself, the easier it is to detach from external opinions. Seeking guidance or advice from others is valuable, but letting judgment dictate your choices is limiting.

Your Inner Critic: The True Source of Judgment Fear

Psychologists have found that the fear of external judgment often stems from self-judgment (Marando, 2020). Many of us have an inner critic—an internal voice that scrutinizes our actions, performance, and self-worth. This self-criticism can be relentless. It can shape our fears and make us believe that others see us as harshly as we see ourselves.

Think about it: When you're confident in something, do you worry about being judged? Likely not. It's when you doubt yourself that the fear of judgment becomes paralyzing. The truth is, we project our insecurities onto others, assuming they see our flaws as clearly as we do.

As author Louise Hay once said, "You've been criticizing yourself for years, and it hasn't worked. Try approving of yourself and see what happens" (Marando, 2020).

Self-judgment rarely serves us in the long run. While it might create short-term motivation, over time, it erodes self-esteem and reinforces self-doubt. The way you speak to yourself becomes part of your identity, shaping how you present yourself to the world. Instead of fixating on flaws, acknowledge your strengths. Be kind to yourself, and recognize the progress you make, no matter how small.

The Spotlight Effect: People Notice You Less Than You Think

One of the biggest reasons we fear judgment is something called the spotlight effect—the tendency to believe that people are paying much more attention to us than they actually are. This is a common cognitive bias, especially for teens, because at this stage, social belonging feels crucial.

Have you ever walked into a room and felt like everyone was staring at you, analyzing your every move? Or maybe you tripped over your own feet and were convinced the entire class saw it happen? The truth is, most people didn't even notice—or if they did, they forgot about it within minutes.

Studies in psychology confirm this. In one experiment, researchers asked participants to wear an embarrassing T-shirt, like a cringey, outdated pop star, and estimated how many people in the room would notice it. Participants assumed nearly 50% of people would see and judge their shirt. In reality, less than 20% even noticed (Gibson, 2024).

This shows that while we think people are constantly evaluating us, they're usually too busy worrying about themselves. Just like you're focused on how you look, sound, or act, everyone else is also caught up in their own thoughts and insecurities.

How to Use the Spotlight Effect to Your Advantage

Next time you feel anxious about being judged, remind yourself: People aren't watching as closely as you think. Most of your "awkward moments" aren't even memorable to others.

Breaking Free From the Fear of Judgment

You cannot live a fulfilling life while chasing universal approval. It's impossible to please everyone. Instead, focus on aligning with your own values and aspirations.

Overcoming the fear of judgment requires mindfulness and self-acceptance. Pay attention to your thoughts and emotions. Where does your fear originate? How can you challenge it? The process takes time and effort, but the power to break free lies within you.

If you allow your happiness to depend on external opinions, your life will always be dictated by others. Instead, invest in your confidence, self-worth, and personal growth. You are the only one who can define your path. Let go of judgment, embrace who you are, and step forward with courage.

Small, Manageable Steps to Boost Confidence

Overcoming the fear of judgment and social anxiety doesn't happen overnight. Confidence isn't something you either have or don't have—it's a skill you build over time. The key is to take small, manageable steps that gradually push you beyond your comfort zone.

The Power of Gradual Exposure: Facing Social Situations at Your Own Pace

Jumping straight into intimidating situations can feel overwhelming. Instead of forcing yourself into high-pressure interactions, try gradual exposure—small steps that gently stretch your comfort zone.

Let's talk about some ideas:

- If socializing makes you anxious, start by making brief eye contact and smiling at a stranger.

- If speaking up in class feels overwhelming, begin by answering a yes-or-no question instead of giving a full explanation.

- If sharing your work online feels scary, start by posting something small—a single thought, a comment, or a short post—before working up to bigger content.

Each step builds resilience, making the next one easier. Over time, what once felt impossible becomes second nature.

Building Social Confidence Through Micro-Wins

Confidence grows through micro-wins—small achievements that prove to yourself that you're capable. Each time you step outside your comfort zone, even in small ways, it's a victory!

Some examples of micro-wins are:

- initiating a short conversation with a coworker

- giving an opinion in a group discussion

- ordering food without overthinking how you sound

- posting a comment in an online forum

- standing tall and making eye contact in social settings

The more micro-wins you collect, the more your brain recognizes that you can handle social situations. Over time, these small victories add up to significant confidence.

Tracking Your Progress: A Self-Check-In System to Celebrate Small Victories

A great way to stay motivated is by tracking your progress. Keep a simple log or journal where you note down the following:

- a small risk you took today

- how it felt before and after

- what you learned from the experience

For example, you can write something around this: "Spoke up in class today! I was nervous beforehand, but once I did it, I realized no one judged me. It felt empowering."

This practice reinforces your growth, helping you see how far you've come. Confidence isn't about eliminating fear—it's about acting despite it.

Role-Playing for Confidence

Role-playing is a technique where you act out different social situations to practice communication skills, build confidence, and prepare for real-life interactions. It's like a rehearsal for social settings—you get to try different approaches in a safe, low-pressure environment before encountering them in the real world.

By stepping into different roles, you can explore how conversations might unfold, experiment with responses, and become more comfortable handling various scenarios. Whether you're practicing introductions, joining a group conversation, or handling awkward moments, role-playing can help you feel more prepared and self-assured.

Are you ready to get started?

Steps to Role-Play

Role-playing is just like a fun game—it's a way to practice social situations without the pressure of real-life stakes. Think of it as a rehearsal where you can test out different approaches, laugh at the awkward moments, and refine your skills. To play, follow these simple steps:

1. Choose a trusted person—a friend, family member, or mentor who makes you feel safe.

2. Start with easy scenarios and gradually try more challenging ones.

3. Switch roles! Let the other person be the nervous one sometimes.

4. After each round, talk about what worked and what could be improved.

The goal isn't to be perfect—it's to get comfortable with discomfort. The more you practice, the more natural social interactions will feel, making real conversations way easier.

Practicing Conversations in a Low-Pressure Setting

Before facing real-world situations, practicing in a controlled, judgment-free environment can help you feel at ease. Here are some different scenarios to role-play:

Scenario 1: Talking to New People

Starting a conversation can feel nerve-wracking, but simple openers help. Practice introducing yourself: "Hey, I don't think we've met before! It is nice to meet you!" You can then introduce yourself by sharing your name and asking for theirs. Or use an observation: "That's a cool backpack—where did you get it?" Focus on active listening and follow-up questions to keep the conversation going. Try different openers to see what feels natural.

Scenario 2: Joining a Group Conversation

Approaching a group? Listen first, then jump in naturally. Use echoing: "Oh, you're talking about Taylor Swift's new album? I just heard to it, too!" Or ask a follow-up question: "What's your favorite song?" If no one responds immediately, stay relaxed—confidence matters more than speed.

Scenario 3: Handling Awkward Silences

Silences happen! Stay calm and restart the conversation with a comment, such as, "Wow, this coffee shop is busy today." Ask a simple question, such as, "Got any fun weekend plans?" Or use humor, like, "Well, that was a dramatic pause—what were we saying?" Lightheartedness helps ease tension.

Scenario 4: Responding to a Mean Comment

Unfortunately, not every social interaction is positive, and learning how to handle rude or judgmental comments with confidence is important. In this role-play, your partner will pretend to make an unkind remark (without being personal, just for practice). The goal is to explore different responses and find what works best for you.

One option is to confidently ignore the comment and move on, showing that their words don't affect you. If you feel the need to address it, setting a clear boundary can be effective. It can be as simple as: "Hey, I don't think that's cool to say." For situations where humor feels like the right approach, you might try responding with a witty remark: "Wow, did you practice that line in the mirror this morning?" The key is to respond in a way that makes you feel strong rather than small. Practicing different reactions can help you feel more prepared if you ever face a similar situation in real life.

Shifting Focus on the Other Person

When we focus inward, it's easy to get caught up in the spiral of overthinking. But when we take a step back and start thinking about the other person, it helps us step out of our own head and into the present moment. It also shifts our perspective. Instead of worrying about how we're coming across, we start thinking, *What can I learn about this person? What makes them tick? What are they passionate about?* This change in focus allows us to experience social interactions with more ease and enjoyment.

By focusing on the other person, we begin to feel more relaxed, which is a natural antidote to anxiety. And this shift can help you feel more grounded in conversations.

The Art of Active Listening

Active listening can completely transform conversations. It's about genuinely understanding what the other person is saying, rather than just waiting for your turn to talk. Active listening helps you engage in meaningful exchanges and minimizes your own anxious thoughts. It shows the other person that you care, creating a sense of connection that can make both of you feel more comfortable.

Here are some ways to practice active listening:

- **Give your full attention to the speaker.** Put your phone down, make eye contact, and lean in slightly to show you're engaged.

- **Reflect and clarify when needed.** If you're unsure about something, ask follow-up questions like "Can you tell me more about that?" or "What happened next?"

- **Avoid interruption.** Let the other person finish before responding. It shows respect for their words.

- **Be mindful of body language.** Your body language, such as nodding and smiling, shows the other person that you are actively listening and involved in the conversation.

When you actively listen, your mind has less room to focus on worries and fears. Instead, you're involved in the conversation, which takes the pressure off you.

Conversation Starters: Breaking the Ice

Starting a conversation can feel intimidating, but having a few go-to questions can make it easier. The key is to ask questions that are open-ended and allow for natural follow-up.

Here are some conversation starters for different situations:

If you are meeting someone new, you can use these:

- "What's something you've been really into lately?"

- "Do you have any favorite hobbies or things you like to do in your free time?"

- "Are you from around here, or did you move here recently?"

These questions invite the other person to share more about themselves, giving you a chance to learn about their interests and background.

If you are at school or doing group work, ask this:

- "What's the most interesting project or assignment you've worked on recently?"

- "Do you have any tips for staying focused during class?"

- "What's one thing you're looking forward to this semester?"

These help you connect on a school-related level while keeping the conversation light and easygoing.

If you are with a friend who's been quiet or distant, try asking:

- "You've seemed a little off lately. Is everything okay?"

- "I miss hanging out with you. Is there anything on your mind?"

- "You don't have to talk about it if you're not ready, but I'm here if you need someone to listen."

These questions show that you care and are offering a safe space without pushing too hard.

Finding Common Ground

One of the most effective ways to connect with someone is to find common ground. This doesn't mean you have to have everything in common, but it's about discovering shared interests, experiences, or values. When you find something in common, it creates an immediate bond that makes both of you feel more comfortable.

Start by exploring simple, universal topics, such as hobbies or interests, current events or pop culture, or shared experiences, including school, sports, or community events.

For example, if you both love reading, you can ask, "What's the best book you've read lately?" or "Do you prefer fiction or non-fiction?" Sharing your thoughts on a subject creates natural pathways for conversation and helps build rapport.

Even if you don't have a lot in common, focusing on what you do share can ease anxiety and make the interaction feel more natural. You'll find that connection doesn't always require deep, life-altering common ground—it can often be as simple as a shared love for a TV show or a favorite snack.

Start Slow, Start Today

Conquering social anxiety doesn't happen overnight. It's a process, and the best way to begin is by taking small steps. You don't have to suddenly become the life of the party or have perfect conversations. Instead, focus on one interaction at a time, using the tools we've covered to help ease your anxiety and build your confidence.

Today, try to shift your focus away from worrying about yourself and practice becoming genuinely curious about others. Start with something simple, like a friendly question to a classmate or someone in your social circle. It could be as easy as asking about their weekend or how they're managing schoolwork. Let the conversation flow naturally, and allow yourself to be present in the moment.

Every conversation is a chance to practice. Don't put pressure on yourself to perform. Just listen, ask questions, and let the interaction unfold. With each step, you'll start to feel more at ease in social situations.

And most importantly, be kind to yourself. Social anxiety is tough, but it's something you can navigate. Every small victory, every time you choose curiosity over fear, is progress. Over time, these moments will build into something powerful: the confidence to connect, to engage, and to step outside of your comfort zone.

Now, as you take that first step, keep in mind that the next chapter will help you build emotional resilience—the inner strength you need to handle whatever life throws at you. And as you become more resilient, your ability to manage anxiety will only grow stronger!

Chapter 7: Becoming Emotionally Resilient

Ava and Riley both wake up to the same dreaded sound— their alarm clock buzzing like an angry bee. It's Monday, and neither of them is particularly excited about it. But how their days unfold couldn't be more different.

Ava's Monday

Ava groans, slaps the snooze button (twice), and drags herself out of bed, already dreading the day ahead. She remembers she has a big presentation in English class, and her stomach twists into knots. *I'm going to mess it up*, she thinks. *Everyone's going to notice if I say something stupid.* By the time she gets to school, her brain is already spiraling.

Then, things go from bad to worse. She spills coffee on her shirt. A teacher calls on her when she wasn't focused. And the presentation? She stumbles over her words and hears someone giggle. That's it. Game over. She spends the rest of the day replaying every embarrassing moment, convinced she'll never live it down. By the time she gets home, she just wants to crawl under a blanket and pretend the day never happened.

Riley's Monday

Now, let's talk about Riley. She also wakes up feeling groggy, and she's not thrilled about Monday either. But when she remembers her presentation, she reminds herself, *I've practiced. It might not be perfect, but I'll do my best.*

On the way to school, she spills coffee on her shirt too—same unfortunate stain, same Monday chaos. But instead of panicking, she laughs it off and ties her hoodie around her waist. "Could've been worse," she jokes to herself.

In class, when her teacher calls on her unexpectedly, she doesn't know the answer right away. But instead of freaking out, she says, "I have no idea, but now I'm curious." A few people laugh, but not in a mean way. It's just a moment, and it passes.

During her presentation, she stumbles on a word, but she keeps going. And when she hears a giggle from the back of the room, she doesn't assume the worst. Maybe they're laughing at something else. Maybe they're just nervous, too. Either way, she pushes through and finishes strong.

By the time Riley gets home, she's tired, but she's not beating herself up. Yeah, the day had its hiccups, but she handled them. She shrugs it off, grabs a snack, and moves on.

The difference between them is emotional resilience.

Ava and Riley had the *exact* same Monday—the same challenges, the same little disasters. But while Ava let each moment tear her down, Riley bounced back. She didn't take things personally. She didn't let a bad moment turn into a bad day.

That's emotional resilience. It's not about avoiding stress, failure, or awkward moments—it's about handling them in a way that doesn't wreck your confidence. And the good news? Just like any skill, you can build resilience, train it, and get better at it.

So, in this chapter, let's talk about how to become emotionally resilient.

What Is Emotional Resilience and Why Does It Matter?

Emotional resilience is a superpower. It helps you handle stress, setbacks, and challenges without letting them overwhelm you. It means bouncing back from tough situations instead of getting stuck in negative emotions.

It's not about never feeling anxious, sad, or frustrated—it's about how you respond to those feelings. Resilient people acknowledge their emotions, but they don't let them take over. They adapt, learn, and keep moving forward.

And why does it matter? Because life is unpredictable—one minute, you're confidently answering a question in class, and the next, you realize you've had spinach in your teeth all day. There will be awkward moments, stressful tests, friendship drama, and times when absolutely nothing seems to go your way.

Resilience makes sure those moments don't define you. Instead of spiraling into self-doubt and mentally replaying that awkward handshake-hug mix-up 500 times, you learn, grow, and come out stronger, and maybe just double-check the mirror next time.

Seven C's of Emotional Resilience

Let me tell you about my hardworking yet anxious friend, Aria. Aria was dedicated to everything she did—her art, her studies, her volunteer work—but beneath the surface, there was a constant hum of anxiety, a nagging voice that told her she wasn't good enough, that she'd fail, that everything would crumble.

This week, it was her art portfolio. The deadline was fast approaching, and every brushstroke felt like a judgment, every sketch a potential disaster. Her room, usually a vibrant space of creativity, was now a battleground of crumpled paper and half-finished canvases. Can you imagine?

One day, after hearing her sigh in frustration for what felt like the hundredth time, I decided to step in. "Aria," I said, "I know you're overwhelmed, but have you ever heard of the seven C's of emotional resilience?"

She shook her head, so I took a moment to walk her through each one, hoping it would help her manage the anxiety and give her a sense of control over the process:

First, **competence**. "You've worked hard on this," I reminded her. "Think about how far you've come with your art. You've developed your skills, you've practiced, and you've received feedback. You are competent, and that's something to be proud of."

Next, I talked to her about **confidence**. "It's okay to feel nervous. But remember, you've prepared. Trust your process. Art is subjective, and your unique perspective has value. You can trust yourself."

Then, we moved to **connection**. "Remember, you're not alone in this," I said. "Think of your art teacher, Ms. Ramirez, who always encourages you. Your family loves and supports you. You have a whole team behind you, even when it feels like you're facing this alone."

When she looked unsure, I reminded her of **character**. "You are creative, resilient, and capable. Anxiety is just a feeling, not who you are. You've handled challenges before, and you will handle this one, too."

We paused for a moment, and I asked her, "Why are you doing this?" That's when we talked about **contribution**. "Your art is not just about you," I said. "It's about expressing yourself and sharing your vision with others. You have something important to say, and people will connect with that."

We touched on **coping** next. "It's okay if things don't go perfectly. You can handle setbacks. Take breaks when you need to, listen to music, and remember that mistakes are part of the process. Just keep moving forward."

Finally, I reminded her about **control**. "You can't control what everyone thinks, but you can control your effort, your attitude, and how you present your work. Focus on what you can manage, and let go of the rest."

The day of the portfolio review arrived. Aria's heart was beating fast, but she took a deep breath while remembering everything we talked about. She presented her work. Her voice was a little shaky at first, but she found her rhythm as she spoke passionately about her inspiration. She answered questions with confidence, and her enthusiasm was contagious.

When the review ended, Aria felt a sense of accomplishment. The feedback wasn't perfect, but she had presented her work authentically and with confidence. She'd faced her anxiety and found her inner strength.

Aria realized that being hardworking didn't mean being immune to anxiety—it meant having the tools to navigate it, to find her center, and to remember her worth. And with the seven C's, she now knew she always had a toolkit within reach.

Just like Aria, you can take control of your own anxiety and challenges by embracing the seven C's of emotional resilience (Naluri, n.d.). Whether you're facing a big presentation, a creative project, or simply navigating life's uncertainties, these tools are always within your reach. You don't have to face it alone—you have the power to build your own resilience and find your inner strength.

The question, then, is how to become more emotionally resilient, keeping in mind these seven C's. I have two suggestions for you: The pause, plan, proceed method and the 90-second rule.

The Pause, Plan, Proceed Method

Sometimes, emotions hit hard—like when someone says something rude, your parents lecture you for no reason (or at least that's how it feels), or you get a text that makes your stomach drop. Your first instinct might be to react immediately—snapping back, shutting down, or making a quick decision that you'll later regret. That's where the pause, plan, proceed method comes in. It helps you slow down, think things through, and respond in a way that actually helps instead of making things worse.

Pause

Before reacting, stop for a moment. Take a deep breath. If you need more time, excuse yourself: Grab a drink of water, step outside, or just take a second to collect your thoughts. The goal is to create space between the feeling and the reaction.

Plan

Now that you're not running on pure emotion, ask yourself this:

- *What's the best way to handle this?*

- *Do I need to speak up? Walk away? Take a break before responding?*

- *Will my response make things better or worse?*

If you're in a heated conversation, this might mean choosing your words carefully instead of blurting out something you'll regret. If you're dealing with stress, it could mean figuring out a productive next step instead of panicking.

Proceed

Now that you've thought it through, move forward with a response that keeps you in control of the situation—not your emotions. This doesn't mean suppressing your feelings; it just means choosing a response that actually helps. Whether it's calmly explaining your side, setting a boundary, or deciding not to engage at all, you're making a choice that works in your favor.

This method works everywhere—friendships, school stress, family arguments, even those moments when you're about to fire off a risky text. Instead of reacting impulsively and making things worse, you regain control, protect your energy, and handle things in a way that leaves you feeling proud, not regretful.

The 90-Second Rule

Brain scientist and author of *My Stroke of Insight*, Jill Bolte Taylor, introduces what she calls the 90-second rule. She explains that when we experience an emotional reaction to something in our environment, a biochemical process is triggered in the brain that lasts for approximately 90 seconds. After that, any lingering emotional response is no longer the result of the initial trigger but a choice to remain in that emotional state (Robinson, 2020).

This means that while we may not have control over our immediate emotional reactions, we *do* have control over how long we let them dictate our state of mind. Once the physiological response subsides, it is our thoughts—our interpretation of the event and our willingness to dwell on it—that keep the emotion alive.

How to Apply the 90-Second Rule in Daily Life

If you feel overwhelmed by anger, anxiety, frustration, or sadness, you can use the 90-second rule as a way to manage your reaction instead of being consumed by it. Here's how:

Step 1: Observe Without Reacting

Instead of immediately acting on the emotion, simply observe it. Notice where you feel it in your body. Is your heart racing? Are your shoulders tense? Pay attention without trying to suppress or amplify the feeling.

Step 2: Breathe Through the 90 Seconds

Take slow, deep breaths. Remind yourself that this is a natural chemical process that will pass on its own in about a minute and a half. Focus on your breath rather than the emotion.

Step 3: Avoid Feeding the Emotion With More Thoughts

After 90 seconds, the biochemical reaction fades, but if you continue replaying the event in your mind, you keep the emotional response alive. Choose to shift your focus instead of ruminating on what happened.

Step 4: Redirect Your Energy

Once the 90 seconds pass, take a constructive action. Stretch, take a short walk, listen to music, or engage in a calming activity that helps you move forward instead of staying stuck.

By practicing the 90-second rule, you can develop greater emotional resilience. You don't have to be controlled by your emotions—you can acknowledge them, let them pass, and decide how to respond with clarity and intention.

The Role of Self-Compassion in Managing Anxiety

By now, we know that anxiety often thrives on self-criticism. When you're feeling overwhelmed, your inner dialogue can quickly become harsh, which reinforces feelings of inadequacy or fear. Self-compassion, however, offers a powerful antidote. Instead of judging yourself for feeling anxious, self-compassion encourages you to respond with kindness, understanding, and patience—just as you would with a close friend in distress.

One simple way to cultivate self-compassion when facing anxiety is through the "What would you say to a friend?" exercise.

The "What Would You Say to a Friend?" Exercise

When you're feeling anxious, take a moment to step outside of your inner dialogue and imagine a close friend experiencing the same struggle. What would you say to them? How would you reassure them? Would you tell them they're failing, or would you remind them that they're doing their best?

Here's how to apply this exercise effectively:

1. **Identify the anxious thought.** Write it down or say it out loud. For example: *I'll never be able to finish this project. I'm not good enough.*

2. **Imagine a friend saying the same thing.** Picture someone you care about expressing this worry to you.

3. **Offer them reassurance.** What would you say to comfort and support them? Maybe you'd remind them of their strengths, their past successes, or simply that they don't have to be perfect.

4. **Turn that kindness toward yourself.** Now, say those same words to yourself. Repeat them until they sink in.

By shifting your perspective, you train your brain to replace self-judgment with self-compassion, helping you break the cycle of anxiety.

The Comfort Habit

Sometimes, managing anxiety isn't just about thoughts—it's also about actions. The comfort habit is a simple, intentional routine that soothes your nervous system and provides a sense of safety. It's a personal ritual that signals to your mind and body that you are okay, even in moments of stress.

A comfort habit could be any of the following:

- wrapping yourself in a cozy blanket with a warm drink

- taking five deep breaths while placing a hand on your heart

- listening to calming music or a favorite podcast

- holding a grounding object, like a smooth stone or a piece of jewelry

- or practicing a gentle stretch or mindful movement

The key is consistency—repeating a small, comforting action teaches your brain that you have tools to manage anxiety, building resilience over time.

By combining self-compassion, the "What would you say to a friend?" exercise, and a personalized comfort habit, you create a supportive system that helps you navigate anxiety with greater ease and kindness.

Create Your Resilience Toolbox

A resilience toolbox is a personalized collection of strategies, reminders, and objects that help you manage anxiety and regain a sense of balance. Think of it as a set of tools you can turn to whenever you feel overwhelmed. The key is to include a mix of mental, emotional, and physical tools that work best for you.

Choose One Strategy for Each Category

For **mindset tools**, you can:

- Repeat a mantra to anchor yourself in the present moment and reinforce your inner strength. Such as saying *I am capable and resilient* to yourself.

- Or use a journal to write down anxious thoughts and actively reframe them with a more supportive perspective.

For **action-based tools**, you can:

- Hold a physical object, like a worry stone, stress ball, or a comforting piece of fabric, to bring focus and calm during anxious moments.

- Or create a list of go-to calming activities such as stretching, doodling, taking a walk, or organizing a small space to redirect your energy.

For **emotional support tools**, you can:

- Write a letter to yourself that reminds you of past victories and reassures you that you have overcome challenges before and will again.

- Or create a playlist of calming or empowering songs to shift your emotional state and provide comfort during stressful times.

Personalize and Keep It Accessible

Once you've selected your tools, gather them in a small box, notebook, or digital note. The idea is to make them easily accessible so that when anxiety strikes, you don't have to think—you just reach for your toolbox.

Try It in Real Time

The next time you feel overwhelmed, pick one tool from each category and use it. Over time, you'll refine your toolbox, keeping what works and replacing what doesn't.

By building and using your Resilience Toolbox, you create a reliable system for managing stress, increasing emotional strength, and reminding yourself that you have the power to bounce back.

You are unstoppable, and you've got this!

Our next and final chapter talks about friendships and boundaries because "No" is a complete sentence!

Ever had a friend who leaves you feeling like you just ran a marathon... emotionally? Yeah, we're tackling that. We'll break down healthy versus toxic dynamics (so you can spot the energy vampires), learn to set boundaries without the guilt trip, and discover how to build friendships that energize instead of exhaust you. Because life's too short for drama—let's keep the good vibes only!

Chapter 8: Friendships and Boundaries—How to Avoid Anxiety-Triggering Relationships

Aizel used to love hanging out with her best friend, Chloe. They had inside jokes, spent hours texting, and always partnered up for group projects. But lately, something felt off. Chloe had started making little jabs at Aizel—comments like, "Wow, you're really wearing that?" or "I guess not everyone can be good at math." Aizel laughed them off at first, but the words stuck with her. She started second-guessing her outfits, hesitating before raising her hand in class.

It wasn't just the comments. Chloe expected Aizel to be available 24-7, blowing up her phone with texts and getting upset if Aizel didn't reply immediately. If Aizel made plans with other friends, Chloe would send guilt-tripping messages like, "I guess I'm not important to you anymore."

The anxiety crept in slowly. Aizel started checking her phone obsessively, worried she'd miss a text and upset Chloe. When she saw Chloe's name pop up on her screen, her heart raced. She spent hours overthinking every reply, trying to keep the peace. Even when they weren't talking, Aizel couldn't relax. She caught herself replaying conversations in her head, wondering if she had done something wrong.

Aizel didn't know what to do. The thought of confronting Chloe made her chest tighten—what if it made things worse? But pretending everything was fine wasn't working either. No matter what she did, she felt anxious. Was she overreacting? Or was this friendship hurting her more than helping her?

Aizel's situation isn't uncommon. Friendships are supposed to make you feel supported, happy, and safe. Sometimes, though, they can do the exact opposite. A friendship that causes constant stress, self-doubt, or guilt can take a serious toll on your anxiety levels. The good news? You have more control over your friendships than you might think! In this chapter, let's focus on building friendships that actually help you feel good—not ones that leave you emotionally drained.

Identifying Toxic vs. Healthy Friendships

Friendships play a huge role in your mental and emotional well-being. A good friend can make a bad day better, cheer you on when you need it most, and be a safe space where you can truly be yourself. On the other hand, a toxic friendship can leave you feeling exhausted, anxious, or even questioning your own self-worth. But how do you tell the difference?

What Makes a Healthy Friendship?

A great friendship isn't just about having fun together—it's about feeling safe, respected, and valued. Here are some key signs of a healthy friendship:

Mutual Support: Friends Who Lift You Up, Not Drag You Down

Imagine you just found out you got a role in the school play, or you aced a difficult test. A good friend would celebrate with you—maybe send an excited text or hype you up in person. They'd be genuinely happy for you.

Now imagine the opposite: You share your good news, and your friend brushes it off, changes the subject, or even makes a sarcastic comment like, "Must be nice to be lucky all the time." That's not support—that's minimizing your achievements.

Mutual support means you do these things:

- encourage each other's successes instead of feeling jealous

- be there during tough times instead of disappearing when things get hard

- listen when the other person needs to vent, without making it all about themselves

A real friend makes you feel confident, heard, and valued—not like your feelings and achievements don't matter!

Trust and Respect: The Foundation of Every Strong Friendship

Think about someone you truly trust. If you tell them something personal, do you worry that they'll gossip about it later? If you make a mistake, do they hold it against you or understand that nobody's perfect?

Trust and respect go hand in hand. They form the foundation of a healthy friendship. Honesty is key—your friend tells you the truth, even when it's difficult, but always with kindness. For example, if you have something stuck in your teeth, they'll let you know right away, sparing you any embarrassment. They also keep promises, never canceling plans last minute without a good reason or sharing your secrets with others. Respecting boundaries is another essential aspect of a strong friendship—they never pressure you into doing something you're uncomfortable with or invade your personal space. Together, these elements create a bond built on mutual understanding and care.

Without trust and respect, a friendship can start to feel like walking on eggshells—never sure if you're being judged, talked about behind your back, or pressured into something you don't want to do. However, a great friend helps with anxiety because you know they're there as your support system—you don't need to worry about things so much!

Emotional Safety: Feeling Free to Be Yourself

A good friendship should feel like a safe space, not a constant source of stress. You should be able to share your thoughts and feelings without the fear of being left out, mocked, or judged.

If you feel like you have to constantly filter what you say, laugh off rude comments, or "play it cool" to avoid upsetting your friend, it's worth asking yourself: *Is this friendship actually making me happy?*

Red Flags of Toxic Friendships

Now, we've talked about what to look for in a great friend. However, not all friendships are good for you. While healthy friendships lift you up, toxic ones do the opposite—they drain your energy, make you question yourself, and leave you feeling worse rather than better. The tricky part? Toxic friendships don't always start out that way. They often develop slowly, making it hard to recognize the warning signs until the stress and anxiety become overwhelming.

Here are some key red flags to watch out for:

Lack of Support: When Your Friend Feels More Like a Stranger

A real friend listens, encourages, and stands by you. A toxic friend, on the other hand, may act like they don't care deeply about your struggles. They might make it seem like your feelings are silly or make every conversation about themselves. If you always feel like you're giving but getting little in return, that's a sign your friendship isn't balanced.

Manipulation: When "Friendship" Feels Like a Game

Some friends use guilt or pressure to control your actions. They might say things like, "If you were really my friend, you'd do this for me," or get upset when you spend time with other people. They may also make you feel responsible for their emotions, expecting you to "fix" their problems. True friends respect your choices—they don't manipulate you into doing things their way. You're also not their personal therapist or nanny, and your needs and your family and homework matter, too!

Constant Negativity: A One-Way Street of Complaints

Everyone has tough days, and venting is normal. But if a friend constantly focuses on their problems—without showing interest in yours—it can be exhausting. Worse, some toxic friends bring non-stop negativity, always pointing out what's wrong but never trying to improve things. Over time, this can drag you down emotionally.

Nobody likes a fly that can only see the trash; sometimes, you want to be a butterfly and look for the sunshine and clean, green leaves! Only looking at the trash gives you more reasons to be anxious.

Overstepping Boundaries: When "No" Isn't Respected

Healthy friendships have mutual respect, including respect for boundaries. A toxic friend may push you into situations you're uncomfortable with, come into your personal space, or not leave you in peace when you need alone time. If a friend constantly ignores your feelings or pressures you, that's a red flag. Over time, the pressures can increase your anxiety.

Gaslighting: When a Friend Makes You Question Reality

Gaslighting is when someone makes you doubt your own experiences, saying things like, "You're overreacting," or "That never happened." A toxic friend might rewrite past events, twist your words, or act like your concerns aren't valid. Over time, this can seriously affect your confidence and decision-making.

How Toxic Friendships Can Increase Your Anxiety

Toxic friendships aren't just emotionally exhausting—they can do a real number on your mental health.

Increased Stress: The Emotional Disaster Waiting to Happen

When you're constantly walking on eggshells around a friend, worried about their reaction or feeling drained after every interaction, it triggers stress and anxiety. You might feel on edge, overthink every conversation, or even start dreading messages from them.

Long-Term Effects: The Damage Adds Up

Staying in a toxic friendship for too long can chip away at your self-esteem. If someone regularly makes your feelings sound silly, manipulates you, or makes you feel unimportant, you might start believing that's what you deserve. Over time, this can lead to constant stress, low confidence, and unhealthy coping mechanisms like avoiding social interactions or hiding your emotions. All of this, of course, is terrible for your anxiety levels!

Setting Boundaries Without Guilt

There's a thin line between a good friendship and a bad one. Often, a great friend becomes uncomfortable to be around because they've become *too* close for comfort. Do you know what I mean? If you want to keep a great friendship great, you need boundaries.

Think of boundaries as your personal "rules of the road" for relationships. They help you decide what feels okay and what doesn't. It's like setting a do-not-disturb mode for your well-being. Good boundaries don't push people away; they help you feel safer, more confident, and less overwhelmed.

When you set clear limits, you take charge of your emotional space. This means less stress, fewer awkward situations, and way more self-respect instead of getting drained by negativity and pressure.

Here are a few types of boundaries you might need:

- **Emotional boundaries:** Protecting your feelings by saying no to guilt trips, drama, or constant venting from others

- **Physical boundaries:** Deciding who gets a hug and who gets a wave (because not everyone likes the same level of closeness)

- **Time boundaries:** Making sure you're not overcommitting or saying yes to things that leave you exhausted

- **Digital boundaries:** Controlling who gets access to you online, how often you respond to messages, and when you unplug

Remember, setting boundaries isn't selfish—it's necessary. The people who truly care about you will respect them, and anyone who doesn't? That's a red flag worth noticing.

How to Recognize When Your Boundaries Are Being Crossed

Not all boundary violations are obvious. Sometimes, you don't realize it's happening until you start feeling constantly drained, anxious, or even guilty after spending time with a certain friend. If you find yourself dreading their texts or feeling like you *owe* them your time and energy, that's a red flag.

Here are some scenarios for reference:

- a friend overshares deeply personal issues without checking if you're comfortable

- someone expects constant emotional support but doesn't offer the same in return

- a friend pushes you to hang out or talk when you clearly need space

If any of this sounds familiar, trust your gut. Your feelings are valid, and noticing these patterns is the first step toward protecting your mental well-being. There are many, many scenarios where friends might push your boundaries, so pay attention to your feelings for hints!

How to Set Boundaries Without Feeling Guilty

Setting boundaries can feel awkward at first, especially if you're used to putting others' needs before your own. But boundaries aren't about shutting people out—they're about creating healthy relationships where both people feel respected.

A great way to communicate your needs is by using "I" statements. Instead of saying, "You never give me space," try, "I feel overwhelmed when I don't have time to recharge." This gets your point across without blaming the other person. Remember, saying "no" doesn't have to be harsh or rude. A simple "I can't make it today, but let's plan for another time" is both clear and kind.

When setting boundaries, some friends may push back. They might act hurt, dismiss your needs, or try to guilt-trip you. Stay calm and repeat your boundaries without over-explaining. If someone consistently ignores your limits, it may be a sign that the friendship isn't a healthy one.

What to Do When Conflict Causes Anxiety

For many teens, conflict can feel overwhelming, triggering extreme anxiety. You might even have the urge to shut down completely. However, avoiding tough conversations only builds more stress. Speaking up calmly protects your peace—and your confidence.

Think about this: Would you like to keep being anxious in case your old bestie texts you something personal and hurtful? Or would you rather have one hard, long, clear-cut conversation and try to clean up the mess forever? I vote for Option 2!

Tools for Managing Conflict Without Escalating Anxiety

Ready to solve the problem once and for all? Here are three steps to help:

1. **Stay calm in the moment.** When you feel anxiety creeping in, try deep breathing, counting to ten, or something similar. Give yourself a moment to pause and keep your emotions in check.

2. **Listen before reacting.** Instead of jumping to defend yourself, take time to understand your friend's perspective. Active listening shows you care and helps prevent misunderstandings.

3. **Know when to compromise—and when to stand firm.** Not every disagreement needs to be a battle! Finding a middle ground can strengthen friendships, but if something goes against your values or well-being, it's okay to stand your ground.

How to Rebuild After a Conflict

Conflicts are often great because you put all your problems out there and look for a solution. Even if they feel awful, you can start fresh and set new, better boundaries for an improved friendship. Here's how you can recover after a tough conflict:

- **Healing takes time.** After an argument, give yourself and your friend space to process emotions. Rushing to "fix" things too soon can make tensions worse.

- **Apologize sincerely (if needed).** If you made a mistake, a simple, honest apology—without excuses—can go a long way. Saying, "I'm really sorry for how I reacted. I value our friendship," can help rebuild trust. Excuses, on the other hand, can make things worse!

- **Know when to let go.** If a friendship feels one-sided or toxic or continues to harm your well-being, it may be time to step away. Walking away isn't failure—it's self-respect. Future you will thank current you for cutting out negative influences.

Check It Out With an Activity!

Navigating tough conversations can be nerve-wracking, but a little preparation can make all the difference. Having a mental or written script can help you feel more confident and in control. When you know what you want to say, you're less likely to freeze up, over-explain, or feel anxious or pressured into something uncomfortable.

Here are a few example scenarios with scripts you can personalize:

- **When a friend constantly demands your time, you can say:** "I really value our friendship, but I need some time to focus on personal stuff. Let's plan something for next week so I can be fully present."

- **When a friend makes hurtful or passive-aggressive comments, you can say:** "When you said I'm X, it made me feel Y. I'd really appreciate it if we could have more respectful conversations."

- **When a friend is unreliable or cancels plans often, you can say:** "I understand things come up, but this happens a lot. It makes me feel like our plans aren't important. Can we figure out a way that works for both of us?"

Take a moment to personalize these scripts with similar "I" statements. Try saying them out loud in front of a mirror or practicing with a trusted friend. The more you practice, the easier these conversations will become.

Conclusion

For one last time, let's suppose you're in the middle of a big, nerve-wracking moment—maybe it's giving a class presentation, texting someone first, or walking into a room where you don't know anyone. Your heart is racing, your brain is pulling the fire alarm, and anxiety is whispering its usual nonsense: *You're going to mess this up. Everyone will notice. Just don't even try.*

But this time, something different happens.

Instead of spiraling, you remember something from this book. Maybe you use the name-it-to-tame-it trick and say, "Oh hey, anxiety, I see you're back at it again." Maybe you take a deep breath, plant your feet, and remind yourself that discomfort isn't danger. Maybe you think, *Wait a second—I've been through this before, and I survived.*

And then, you do the thing anyway. And guess what? The world *doesn't* end. In fact, you feel a little… proud. A little more in control—because you are.

That's how it happens—one moment at a time, one decision at a time. Anxiety may still pop up because it's persistent like that, but now, you have strategies that work. You've built up skills like a gamer leveling up—self-talk boosts, breathing hacks, perspective shifts, and ways to challenge the lies anxiety tells you. You're not helpless. You're not stuck. You are the main character of your story, and anxiety? It's just a background noise you've learned to tune out.

And remember—progress isn't about never feeling anxious again. It's about facing things that used to scare you and realizing, *Hey, I can handle this.* It's about proving to yourself, again and again, that you're braver than you think.

So, take what you've learned and use it. Try new things. Make mistakes. Laugh at yourself. Be the kind of person who refuses to let fear call the shots. And if you ever need a reminder of how capable you are, just flip back through these pages, take a deep breath, and say, "I've got this." Because you *do*!

Thank you!

If you enjoyed this book, please consider leaving a review on Amazon. Your review can help others struggling with anxiety who could benefit from the strategies shared in this book. Thank you for your support!

References

Ackerman, C. (2017, January 18). *21 mindfulness exercises, techniques & activities for adults.* Positive Psychology. https://positivepsychology.com/mindfulness-exercises-techniques-activities/

Biology of anxiety. (n.d.). Psychology Today. https://www.psychologytoday.com/intl/basics/anxiety/the-biology-of-anxiety

Chaplin, T. M., Gillham, J. E., & Seligman, M. E. P. (2008). Gender, anxiety, and depressive symptoms. *The Journal of Early Adolescence, 29*(2), 307–327. https://doi.org/10.1177/0272431608320125

Comiter, J. (2024, October 16). *10 movies that portray what anxiety is really like.* Verywell Mind. https://www.verywellmind.com/films-about-anxiety-8723579#toc-inside-out-2--jenny-d-25

Gibson, N. (2024, February 12). *Is everyone staring? Why wearing a Barry Manilow t-shirt isn't as embarrassing as we think.* Medium. https://medium.com/@nicolewrites1974/is-everyone-staring-why-wearing-a-barry-manilow-t-shirt-isnt-as-embarrassing-as-we-think-e6c769754052

Hoshaw, C. (2022, March 29). *What mindfulness really means and how to practice.* Healthline.

https://www.healthline.com/health/mind-body/what-is-mindfulness#mindful-therapy

Marando, C. (2020, November 5). *Why we fear other people's judgment.* Medium. https://medium.com/in-fitness-and-in-health/why-we-fear-other-peoples-judgment-and-how-i-m-trying-to-overcome-it-5be5ed12ffac

Naluri. (n.d.). *Thriving through challenges: A guide to the 7 Cs of resilience.* Naluri. https://www.naluri.life/community/articles/thriving-through-challenges-a-guide-to-the-7-cs-of-resilience

Panic attacks & panic disorder. (n.d.). Cleveland Clinic. https://my.clevelandclinic.org/health/diseases/4451-panic-attack-panic-disorder#symptoms-and-causes

Robinson, B. E. (2020, April 26). The 90-second rule that builds self-control. *Psychology Today.* https://www.psychologytoday.com/intl/blog/the-right-mindset/202004/the-90-second-rule-builds-self-control

Smith, J. (2023, November 30). *How to stop a panic attack: 13 effective methods.* MedicalNewsToday. https://www.medicalnewstoday.com/articles/321510#methods

Su'a, J. (2014, July 31). *An epic battle…*. Medium. https://medium.com/@Justinsua/an-epic-battle-7f72f0257bfd

Teenagers and sleep. (2018, November 5). Better Health Channel. https://www.betterhealth.vic.gov.au/health/healthy living/teenagers-and-sleep

www.ingramcontent.com/pod-product-compliance
Ingram Content Group UK Ltd.
Pitfield, Milton Keynes, MK11 3LW, UK
UKHW020726090925
7802UKWH00039B/889